**BE YOUR
OWN LEADER**

ANNELIESE MONDEN
CHANTAL SMEDTS

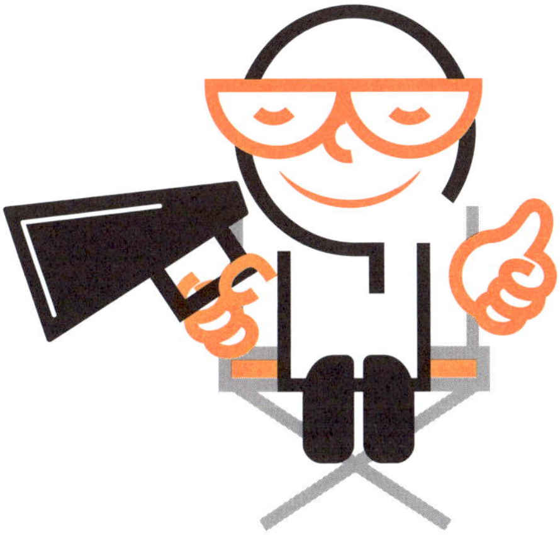

BE YOUR OWN LEADER

AT HOME AND AT WORK

Dedicated to those who have the courage
to take control of their own life.

This book was originally published as *Word je eigen leider. Thuis en op het werk*,
LannooCampus Publishers (2017).

D/2017/45/590 – ISBN 978 94 014 4818 5 – NUR 808

Translation: Ian Connerty
Cover: Gert Degrande | De Witlofcompagnie
Interior design: Wendy De Haes

© Anneliese Monden, Chantal Smedts & Lannoo Publishers nv, Tielt, 2017.

LannooCampus Publishers is a subsidiary of Lannoo Publishers,
the book and multimedia division of Lannoo Publishers nv.

All rights reserved.
No part of this publication may be reproduced and/or
made public, by means of printing, photocopying,
microfilm or any other means, without the prior
written permission of the publisher.

LannooCampus Publishers
Erasme Ruelensvest 179 box 101
3001 Leuven
Belgium
www.lannoocampus.com

CONTENT

INTRODUCTION	8
TIPS FOR THIS BOOK	12

I AM — 15

1. A FIRST CHECK-UP — 16
BORN TO LEAD YOUR OWN LIFE — 16
You are ready to take responsibility for yourself and your actions

DIGEST AND FLUSH — 23
You can only move on if you leave the past behind

2. FIND YOUR PASSION — 31
FIND YOUR FUEL — 32
This is where the search starts for the things that really motivate you

WITH COURAGE TO THE CORE — 35
Gaining insight into your core and what is stopping you from finding it can be deeply confrontational

THE SCRIPT OF YOUR LIFE — 39
There are different ways to discover your drivers, which go far beyond your simple objectives

LIVE YOUR DREAM — 47
Live your dream by turning your drivers into objectives

DRENCH YOUR FILM WITH PASSION — 54
Deal consciously with the things you really want

3. TAKE GOOD CARE OF YOURSELF — 60
WALK YOUR BODY — 60
A chapter full of attention for your body
CHARGE YOUR BATTERIES – OFTEN — 66
Search for your energy givers
SMILE AT YOUR REFLECTION IN THE MIRROR — 72
The effect of a positive self-image
FIND YOUR STOP BUTTON — 79
Sometimes you need to step out of the rat race

4. DON'T LET YOURSELF BE SIDETRACKED — 84
PUT YOURSELF BEHIND THE WHEEL — 84
Live your own life and not someone else's
INSTALL AN ANTI-VIRUS PROGRAMME — 90
Your conversations with yourself have a bigger impact than you think
DON'T CLIMB TOO QUICKLY UP THE LADDER — 95
How prejudices can sabotage you
SEE THE WORLD REGULARLY UPSIDE DOWN — 102
If necessary, look at things from a different angle

YOUR IDENTITY CARD — 107

I DO — 111

1. PRESS THE PLAY BUTTON — 112
AND… ACTION! — 112

2. 'DOING' FOR DUMMIES — 118
UNPLUG YOUR EARPHONES — 118
Listening is more than waiting to respond
PUT ENOUGH QUESTION MARKS IN YOUR SCRIPT — 126
The power of asking the right questions
FEED YOUR FELLOW (WO)MAN — 131
Feedback serves to feed others

3. YOU ARE THE BOSS — 138
LEARN TO SAY 'NO' — 138
How a 'no' can be a 'yes' for you
GET YOUR FRAMES STRAIGHT — 149
Learn to set boundaries

4. TOGETHER WE ARE STRONG — 154
LOOK AT WHAT OTHERS CAN GIVE YOU — 154
Life is about giving and receiving. So make sure you receive!
(NET)WORKING TOGETHER — 160
Together, we can go to the next level

DIRECTOR'S EXAM — 169

FINALLY: GOOD LUCK WITH YOUR PREMIERE! — 173
THANK YOU — 175

INTRODUCTION

Ever since Descartes made his famous statement 'je pense, donc je suis' (I think therefore I am) we have become a little bit misshapen. Our rational thought became so important that everyone's mind began racing. We mapped out the universe, we dissected the human body, we put everything neatly into tables and graphics. Fascinating treatises were written, great philosophies born, erudite intellectual discussions conducted... But there was one thing we overlooked: namely, that a person is much more than his brain box alone; there are also things like heart and intuition. The more we use our head, the more we lose contact with our body and our feelings.

In recent decades, hard- and software were added to the equation. The internet has given us access to unlimited information. We can make an opinion about anything and everything known worldwide. What's more, it all happens much more quickly than ever before. According to Moore's Law (Moore was the founder of Intel), the processing power of a computer doubles every two years. To do what a smartphone can do today, we would have needed a whole room full of computers back in 1980.

The result? Our heads are almost exploding from all the information we nowadays need to assimilate at lightning speed. We are tired out by endless discussions and endless reasoning. We have reached the limits of ever more thought, ever faster action, and ever more efficient living. An unpleasant feeling of emptiness seems to be creeping up on us, slowly but surely.

That feeling is strengthened by the high level of expectation placed on us by others, by society and by ourselves. We want a diploma, a well-paid job, a warm family, three holidays a year, membership of a fitness club, a marathon medal and, if at all possible, to dine out at least twice a week. We are constantly on the move, trying to fulfil five roles at once, and we are so focused on what we are doing that we actually lose ourselves in the trivia of the day. Before we know it, we are simply living to achieve all the many different things that are expected of us, even though we have long forgotten who or what is at the basis of those expectations. We are no longer in control of our own lives.

Do you recognize a number of these things? There is a good chance that you do. Our aim in this book is to help you press the 'stop' button. We want to take time to get back to basics. Who are we, really? What motivates us? What do we want to achieve? What makes us feel good? What is important? These questions may seem simple, but the answers often lay buried deep inside us. You would be amazed how many people never think about these key life issues. And that's why burn-outs are so common today. This book will show you how to develop the resilience you need to take back and retain control of your life, even in difficult times.

In the first part – 'I am' – we will pause to consider at some length exactly how you can discover the core of your being. This is a necessary exercise. Because if you don't know who you are, what you want and what you believe in, you are drifting rudderless through life, irrespective of all the impulses and expectations that bombard you daily. You are no longer leading your own life. You no longer know what is essential and what is irrelevant. You no longer know where your priorities lie. As a result, you will find it more and more difficult to make the important decisions that can move your life in the direction you want it to go.

It will only be at the end of part 1 that you will be able to properly fill in your new identity card, with head held high and both feet firmly on the ground. At that moment, it will be no problem for you to say with confidence 'I am...'

In part two – 'I do' – we will teach you how to become your own leader, the director in the film of your own life. The objective is simple: with your identity card in your pocket, we are going to take a walk through every aspect of your life and check to make sure that your actions, your daily activities and your relations with others are as well attuned as they possibly can be to who you really are. Because it is only when your being and everything you do are in perfect harmony that you will be able to feel really happy and successful. Only then will you be able to exude authenticity and leadership.

In this book, we are going to bare our souls. We will commit to a fresh perspective and take inspiration from the start of our life – to when we were still babies. What do babies do? They eat, they drink, they poo. When something is wrong, they cry. But when they start to realize that interaction with others can be fun, they begin to laugh. That, in all simplicity, is what being human is all about. And that will be our starting point.

With this book, we want to help you to become the leader of your own life. But who is 'we', exactly? We are Anneliese Monden and Chantal Smedts, the inspiration behind the Qlick coaching company. For more than 10 years we have been guiding people who want to work at improving their personal development. To make this possible, we too have had a long way through the same process, to reach the point where we can be passionately engaged in doing the things we really love. We are both highly driven, but with different backgrounds: the one a leader in a large multinational, the other an entrepreneur and owner of a flourishing business with several branches. We combined our different experiences and life lessons to create a coaching trajectory that we would now like to share with you in this book. In doing so, we will not simply be following the highway of reason, but will also be taking detours into fascinating, unexpected and slightly less logical byways.

In other words, this book will be your coach. It is a 'be-and-do' book, which will show you how to achieve greater authenticity and self-confidence. It will help you to increase your resilience and allow you to make important decisions in keeping with who you really are. Perhaps you are considering a career switch? Or maybe you want to improve your communication with others? Perhaps you are at a crossroads in your personal or professional life? Or maybe you don't feel comfortable with yourself and just want to reflect for a moment about where you are going? Whatever it is, this book can help you to discover the right way.

But be careful: it won't be easy to find the answers you seek and the energy you need. Becoming the leader of your own life demands effort and perseverance. Sometimes it will be necessary to look at yourself critically, rather than looking for excuses in others or in the setbacks you have encountered in the past. You will need to have the courage to move beyond mere reason and learn to trust your intuition, your heart, your gut feeling. Once you are prepared to get down to essentials, we are ready to begin. Coaching starts at the moment when you want and are able to take full responsibility for your own life.

We will give you insights, working methods and exercises based on our experience. We will also take you inside our own coaching practice, with numerous concrete examples from real-life case studies. These are not dramatic stories, but illustrate recognizable, day-to-day situations.

Together with you, we want to discover how you can show others in the most authentic way possible just exactly who you are. For you, 'Je pense, donc je suis' will become 'I do as I am' – and vice versa.

'You are...': that is the starting point.
That is how you become your own leader.

TIPS FOR THIS BOOK

The world around us has become so efficient that it continually pushes you to take action after action, so that you rarely stop to think what is important or who you really are. This book seeks to deliberately reverse that process. It starts with who you are and only then moves on to what you can or should do, because we are convinced that this will make your life simpler and, ultimately, happier. All too often we search for happiness outside ourselves, so that we end up getting lost in the minutiae of the thousand and one things we have to do.

Therefore, we will start with 'I am' (which Michael Hall, Executive Director of the International Meta-Coach System, calls our internal powers) and then go on to 'I do' (the 'external powers', according to Hall).

We make use of the metaphor of a film director, to ask 'who are you as a person?' (I am) and 'how will you direct your film?' (I do). At the end of the road, you will see whether or not you have earned your director's diploma.

MODULE 1: 'I AM'

This is the search for the core of your being, the real 'you'. It starts with the things that are important for you, what motivates you, and how your different objectives in life interact. Each chapter contains a number of insights and tips to help you discover who you are. At the end of each chapter there is a section 'Coach yourself': a series of self-reflection questions that you can also find if you send an email to info@qlick.today.

Module 1 ends with your identity card, in which you can amalgamate all the insights you have learned about who you are. Your identity card mirrors your true identity, the real you: 'I am...'

MODULE 2: 'I DO'

This is all about the things you do, about how you can take action and how you can communicate with others in ways that will move you closer to the real you.

Once again, you will find insights and tips to help you achieve this and a set of self-reflection questions that are also available online.

Module 2 ends with the award of your director's diploma, the skills that you need to lead your own life. You are going on a journey, and you take with you... your identity card and your director's diploma.
Enjoy this wonderful voyage of discovery!

Director: your unique 'you'
Starring: you
Location: your life
Also featuring: the people you meet on the way
Entrance fee: the price you are willing to pay

I AM

My internal strengths
MY IDENTITY

My external strengths
MY DIRECTOR'S DIPLOMA

WHO I REALLY AM, WHAT IS IMPORTANT TO ME,
THE RELATIONSHIP BETWEEN SPIRIT, HEART AND GUT FEELING,
WHAT DRIVES ME (PASSION)
HOW THOUGHTS AND EMOTIONS INFLUENCE ME

1. A FIRST CHECK-UP

Congratulations. The fact that this book is in your hands means that you want to become the director of your own life. But before you can start, you first need to undergo a thorough but necessary check-up, to make sure that this is really something for you…

BORN TO LEAD YOUR OWN LIFE
You are ready to take responsibility for yourself and your actions

 Note to the director
You are ready to follow a trajectory that will allow you to draw up your own identity card. But before you can do that, you need to be certain that you have the right mental attitude for this journey. Because if that's not the case, this book won't work. So make sure you read this chapter carefully before you go any further.

Are leaders born or can you learn how to become a good leader? It is a question that has been asked many times and there are many different answers in the professional literature. To be clear, this is not something we are going to discuss in this book. We are not interested in your calling card or your LinkedIn profile. Our starting point is your life. You were born to lead your own life. In other words, you are already a born leader.

In this sense, leading is much more than just learning a few skills. To take your life fully into your own hands, you need to search for your true identity: this means who you are, not just what you do. You can compare it with a chef. Just because you have a chef's diploma doesn't mean that you will automatically be successful in the world of fine dining. Being able to cook well is certainly a good basis, but if you can also create a story around the food you make, a story that truly reflects who you are and how you live your life, this will not only make people curious but also inspire them. Then the crowds will flock to your restaurant, not only to sample your delicious dishes, but also to see how you have decorated the rooms, how you work in the kitchen, how you respond to your staff and your guests. Then they will buy your cookbooks, not only to try out the recipes at home, but also to learn more about you as a person and your way of life.

WHAT ROLE ARE YOU GOING TO PLAY?

Look at your life as though it is a film and ask which role you want to play. A supporting role? The leading role? Or do you want to be the director? If you have the feeling that you are always doing things that other people have decided for you, then you are really only playing a supporting role in your own life. After a while, this will probably give you an uncomfortable feeling. And so it should. You can hardly be satisfied with such a minor role when you are capable of so much more.

Perhaps you frequently make your own decisions, but find it tiring. In your heart of hearts, you know that you only take those decisions because that is what other people expect of you: your colleagues, your boss, your partner, your friends, your parents. You may be playing a leading role, perhaps even a starring one, but it takes a heavy toll on your strength. It is not always easy to do what others want you to do, often because it is not really what you want to do at all. It is not in keeping with who you truly are. That takes a lot of energy, so in this role you will regularly need time for yourself to rest and recover.

If you are the director of the film of your life, you are in control of everything, so you can make the choices you want to make. You can choose the work you like and how you want to organize it. You can choose the friends you want and decide how to spend the weekend. You determine what is important and what is not. As director, you have the power to decide how every scene in the film of your life will look. If you currently think that your film is not going to be a blockbuster, perhaps it is time to take responsibility and finally sit down in that director's chair.

A LEADER WITH FREEDOM AND RESPONSIBILITY

Directing your own film means more freedom. But it also means more responsibility. If there is a situation in your life you are not happy with, it is the easiest thing in the world to blame someone else. 'I don't feel comfortable in my job, but I only do it because that's what my parents want'; 'I find it hard to complete projects successfully, but that's because my colleagues are always one step ahead of me'. If you always look for the cause of things that are wrong in your life in others or if you expect others to solve your problems for you, then you are actually putting yourself in a victim's role. You are not directing your own film. It is time to stop looking for the answers to your problems outside yourself and start asking how you can do things better or differently.

Directing your own film means more freedom, but also more responsibility.

As director, you need to be responsible for 100% of your film. 95% is not enough. Imagine what might happen if you have no control over that final 5%. What if you forget the lighting? Or forget to order the publicity posters? The consequences of that 'forgotten' 5% can be large and irreversible: booing in the cinemas, not enough people at the box office, financial problems, loss of face and reputation... You can only be satisfied with 100% control. Perhaps you think that 5% is just a small difference, that it's not really important. But imagine that you are trying to read a book and 5% is missing! If you want to make proper use of this book – and direct your film in the best possible way – then only 100% will do. There are no excuses for anything less. Otherwise it will not work.

We would like to illustrate this with an example from our coaching practice. So let us introduce you to Guido. He is fed up, because he has no real satisfaction in his job. So where do you think he is going wrong?

> Guido is down in the dumps. He feels that he is being used at his work and has almost had enough. His boss is always demanding and he seldom gets a compliment, even though he thinks he sometimes deserves one. He mutters to himself: 'My work is not appreciated. My boss is the kind that never gives compliments. But there's nothing to be done, I suppose.' Guido shrugs. 'This is frustrating,' he says. 'I am losing my motivation.'

This fragment is taken from a real-life case study. It illustrates perfectly how people often push the responsibility for their problems onto others. Guido thinks that he does his job well, but it gives him no satisfaction, because he never gets a compliment. Viewed from the perspective of 'take responsibility for your own actions', this is faulty reasoning. Firstly, you are paid to do a good job. That is what every employer expects. In Guido's position, you therefore need to ask yourself if you are doing things right. If the answer is 'yes', you can use this as a source of satisfaction and motivation to do even better. You don't need to wait for confirmation from someone else and you should certainly not assume that your boss is 'not satisfied', simply because you never get a compliment. Maybe he is, as Guido suggests, the kind of man who never gives compliments? Or what if he shows appreciation for your work in a manner that you don't realize or expect? Or perhaps he is simply unaware of how important a few encouraging words can be for people like Guido? That would be a pity, of course, but to use it as a reason for supposing that you are doing something wrong is taking matters too far. If you are someone who needs feedback, then there are other ways of dealing with the situation. Let's look a little further.

> 'What options do you have to change things?' I ask. 'It is what it is,' he answers with a bitter tone in his voice. I say nothing, waiting for my previous question to sink in. I probe a little deeper. 'What about just asking your boss whether or not he is happy with your work? You could

also use the opportunity to tell him what's troubling you.' I can see from Guido's expression that he is digesting what I just said. Slowly, he begins to say: 'Yeees, I suppose I could just ask him what he thinks of my work.' Guido straightens his shoulders and his voice becomes less hesitant. He sees a way to take the situation into his own hands and this is instantly noticeable in his body language.

You can safely assume that everyone has options to bring about change in their life. Of course, blaming someone else means that you don't need (or even see a need) to change or to accept responsibility for your own actions. For many people, this is the easiest solution in the short term. But if you want to be happy in the long term, you need to take yourself out of the victim's role, face up to your responsibilities, take the initiative, decide what you want to do and take action. If you think it is worth

If you want to be happy in the long term, stop playing the victim's role.

changing, then do it consciously and be aware of the likely consequences. If you don't want to change, you need to say that to yourself and accept that you are 100% satisfied with the current situation. But stop pointing the finger at others. They can't live your life for you and they don't determine your happiness. You do that for yourself.

Think about the things that are stopping you from doing this. Is it ignorance, or fear, or laziness, or concern about the possible reaction of those around you? In the final analysis, it doesn't really matter. You no longer need to look to the past. Your future lies ahead of you. All you have to do is dare to take the plunge. The choice is yours.

INNER ACCEPTANCE

We often hear the comment: 'But I don't have the power over all of these things. There are too many other factors involved.' Let's just examine this for a minute. It is true, of course, that you don't always have control over everything that happens to you. For some people things always seem to go right, while for others they always seem to go wrong.

But what you can control is how you react in any given situation. This is what we mean when we say you need to take 100% responsibility.

If you take 100% responsibility, you will soon learn the secret of inner acceptance, no matter what happens. Acceptance is a conscious decision to 'go with the flow'. This gives you new strength to work your way through difficult periods. If, however, you are not able to control your frustration, anger or fear, you will quickly use up all your energy, so that you have none left to help you overcome those moments of stress and strain.

 Jim looks at me. It is his third coaching session. He talks about a company takeover and the restructuring of several other companies. He has big plans, which clearly give him energy. I listen and notice his left hand is shaking. It was something I'd noticed in the previous session as well. Suddenly, Jim stops talking. He looks at me and smiles. 'By the way, I have Parkinson.' The words come easily and spontaneously, as if he is announcing some everyday fact. I am taken by surprise – something that doesn't happen very often. I look at him and see the person, the businessman, the huge energy. At the same time, I discover a little piece of vulnerability that he now wants to share with me.
I have deep respect for the focus he is able to set on the positive things in life.

Jim is an example of someone who is the director of his own life. We can't control what happens to us, but we can control how we react to it. Jim takes 100% responsibility for the things in his life, no matter how difficult they are.

But let's be clear on this point: we are not saying that you should behave like some kind of superhuman, devoid of feelings and emotions. Nor are we saying that you should never be sad or should not show to others that you are going through a grieving process. What we are saying is that if

Many people only take action to change their life after they have been through a dramatic experience. We say: don't wait for it to happen. Take action now.

you live a responsible life, if you do what you like doing, if you are surrounded by the right people, you will develop the resilience to rise above setbacks and sadness, or at least find a way to give them a place. Equally important, this resilience is something you can work at every day. So that you can be strong if something untoward happens tomorrow.

Many people only take action to change their life after they have been through some dramatic experience. We say: don't wait for it to happen. Take action now.

Do you really want to be the director of your own life? If so, you will need to realize that you, and you alone, can create your own happiness. If you are ready to do this, then you are also ready to start your journey with us.

Coach yourself!

What role do you play in your own life?
How do you direct your own life?
What is stopping you from taking 100% responsibility for your life?
When did you last push responsibility for your life onto someone else?
How do you deal consciously with the inner acceptance of difficult situations?
Write down the insights that you will later include in your identity card.

DIGEST AND FLUSH
You can only move on if you leave the past behind

 Note to the director
If you have chosen to more consciously direct your own film from now on, you first need to throw away the old script. It's time to write an updated version. Coaching always starts from now – and it makes no difference whether you coach yourself or are coached by others. If you want to go the extra mile and speed up your personal growth, you need to set off from the situation in which you find yourself today. This obviously doesn't mean that you must ditch everything from the past. There are some elements that you can take with you on your new journey and they will influence how that journey develops. If you want to discover your own core, it is important to be aware of these elements. In this chapter, we will help you to detect them, to digest them and then move on, so that you can begin with a clean slate.

READY TO LET GO?
Many people feel weighed down by their past. The influence of parents and surroundings often has a limiting effect on our own self. We hear people say:
'Am I decisive enough as a leader?'
Yes: you can easily test that for yourself.
Or: 'What will others think?'
Perhaps it might be better to concentrate on what you think.
Or: 'I'm not clever enough to do this.'
Says who (apart from you)? Where is the evidence?

The funny thing is that we often don't know which thoughts are having a limiting effect on us. We regard these thoughts as 'the normal situation', and so we don't recognize them for what they are – whereas for outsiders, who are not troubled by this preconditioning, it is as clear as day that you are a bit of an odd-man-out in this respect. We came across this in our coaching practice with Jacques. He was a successful leader, but was not completely satisfied with the atmosphere in his company.

Jacques: 'I would like to be closer to my staff, connect with them better. But I don't know how. Things are always so busy and I find it difficult to just have a chat without asking about their private life, which seems nosy and impolite.'

Pause. So there you have it: Jacques assumes that it is impolite to ask the people he works with about their private life. But in principle there is nothing wrong with asking your employees and colleagues personal questions, as long as it remains within the bounds of decency. These questions show interest in the other people as persons in their own right, also away from work. But Jacques clearly has difficulty in following this reasoning. So we need to find out where this thought comes from.

Play.

 'You think so?' I ask him.
'Yes, of course,' he replies with conviction. 'You don't do something like that!'
'Really?'
'No, how would you like it if I started asking you those kind of questions?'
I smile and say it would be no problem. If he wants to ask me something, I tell him to just go ahead.
His cheeks turn red with embarrassment: this was not the answer he expected.

It frequently happens that we only realize we are being unnecessarily limited by our own thoughts when someone else points it out to us. Once we are aware of this, we can more easily see where these limiting thoughts came from.

 Suddenly, Jacques turns back towards me, his eyes wider than before... 'Our dad said we couldn't do that,' he whispers. 'He said it time and time again: mind your own business and don't poke your nose into other people's affairs. And whenever someone wanted to give us good advice, he always said: "Who do they think they are? Busybodies!"'

All the pieces of the puzzle slowly fall into place. Jacques realizes that his father's words are still locked inside his head. Of course he doesn't want to be a busybody... But that thought also limits him in his present role as a company leader. He can only move forward if he lets go of those childhood beliefs from the past.

One way or another, we are all programmed. Somewhere between the ages of one year and six years the hard disc in our head is pumped full with all the different impressions we see and hear around us. But it goes even further than that. In systems psychology, it is common practice to look back as far as seven generations to see what kind of mental baggage people are carrying with them from the past. We are then entering the territory of the psychological therapists, who draw up family constellations to confront their patients with members of their family (sometimes in person) to ask them questions about the things they have never previously discussed. Psychotherapy is beyond the scope of a coaching book, but it is important for you to be aware that many of your most deeply held convictions are, in one way or another, inherited from your familial past. In one sense, there is nothing wrong with this; it is perfectly normal – unless, of course, like Jacques, these inherited thoughts have an unconscious limiting effect on you.

BE A FLY ON THE WALL

 You can start to deal with the problem yourself. If you want to learn how to let go, you should do what we call 'the fly on the wall' exercise. Pretend you are a fly, observing your life. A fly cannot feel what you are feeling. It can only watch what is happening around it.

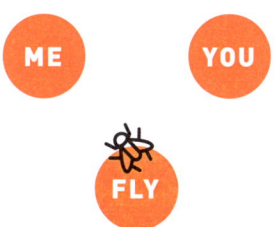

Place three chairs as shown in the above diagram. Think about a conversation you once had when you did not feel comfortable.

Once you have something in mind, go and sit in the 'me' position. Look through your own eyes at your imaginary conversation partner and think about what you felt and experienced at the time. Once you have done this, move across to the chair occupied by the imaginary conversation partner, the 'you' position, and put yourself in their place. Try to look at yourself through their eyes, to experience what you think they must have experienced during the conversation.

Lastly, go and sit on the fly's chair. A fly can only see and hear; it can't feel emotions. Try to imagine what the fly saw and heard, without adding any emotion. What advice would the fly give you? It's quite possible this little insect would offer you new and important insights.

So why not give it a try?

Look at the situations you have encountered in the past, but without judging them, just like the fly does. If you can do this, you will see these situations differently and perhaps, as a result, you will be able to understand them – and the other people involved in them – that much better.

The most fascinating aspect of this process is that you discover lots of interesting things about yourself. For example, you might now see how something that at the time happened almost incidentally actually gave a totally unexpected twist to your life. If you let your past experiences flash through your mind in this way, you will notice that some of them make you smile, while others are much harder to deal with. Your past is a rucksack full of stones that you carry on your back; so make sure that you stop and have a good look at every stone. Each one symbolizes something you have experienced in your life, together with the thoughts associated with those experiences. Imagine that you are taking the stones out of the rucksack one by one, asking the same questions each time:

What incident or event does this stone remind me of?
What emotions did I experience at that time?
Is this thought still of use to me?
Do I still think this thought is right?
Which thought might help me more?

Am I still the same person I was when this event/incident happened? What did this event/incident teach me?

You will soon see that these seemingly simple questions will reveal important insights about who you are. You need these insights if you want to let go of the ones that are limiting you. By throwing away the unnecessary stones that are weighing you down, you will make your rucksack lighter and easier to carry, as well as creating space for new experiences and thoughts.

The stones you keep will be the experiences and thoughts that make you smile or to which you are fondly attached. And you will realize that these stones are not really heavy at all. In fact, they are the building blocks for the new script of your life.

Unless you know how you arrived where you are, you won't know how to move forward.

We seldom take enough time to stop and make an assessment of our life. Yet it is one of the most important things we can do. Unless you can understand how you arrived at the point where you now stand, you will not be able to decide how best to move forward.

DON'T LET YOURSELF BE PARALYZED BY THE PAST

Steven is sitting in front of me. All the sparkle has gone from his eyes. He was once a successful businessman who criss-crossed Europe as a representative for a chemical company. His job was to sell slightly damaged goods to the highest bidder. He had lots of friends and an active social life. That all changed when he reached the age of 45. He had a minor heart attack and the doctor advised him to take things easier. But instead of taking a break and picking up the threads when he was fully recovered, Steven became paralyzed by fear: fear that it would happen again – and that next time it would be worse. He resigned from his job, hardly ever left the house and took no new initiatives whatsoever. At the end of her wits, his wife enrolled him for a series of coaching sessions. And that's how he came to us. From the very

first words he spoke, it was clear that his heart attack was dominating his life. 'I came by train; since my heart attack, I'm scared of driving the car.'
I asked: 'So what brings you here?' Hesitantly, he replied: 'In the first instance, it was my wife's idea. But now I'm here… I want to rediscover my zest for life.'

We all have to deal with difficulties, the scars we carry. Steven is an example of how events from the past – in his case, a heart attack – can paralyze our lives. With every step he took, he thought of nothing but his illness. It was only when he learned how to break this pattern that he was able to move forward again.

Many people get stuck because they allow themselves to be held back by things that happened years ago. Often, it is fear that makes us so powerless to progress. In one sense, this is a natural reaction, which warns us of approaching danger. This is perfectly normal, even beneficial in certain circumstances: life would be very dangerous if we were unable to experience fear. But not if that fear incapacitates our ability to act. So you need to ask yourself whether the fear you feel in any given situation is (still) relevant. Steven could just as easily have reacted in a different way. By taking a rest for a while, he could have been given a renewed boost of energy, allowing him to carry on as before. With a more positive mental attitude, he might have realized that he was lucky to still be alive: he had been given a warning, a warning that should have shown him just how precious life really is.

Negative experiences always leave scars. They are a part of who you are today.

Negative experiences always leave scars. They are a part of who you are today. No more, but also no less. Perhaps you have been through the difficult divorce of your parents, so that your self-confidence was badly dented. Or maybe you grew up in a wealthy family and have never been able to escape from the shadow of your successful father. Or perhaps the opposite is true: your childhood was spent in poverty, so that you now focus on money to the point of exaggeration. External factors influence everyone's lives; they are an integral part of our human experience. You have already come a long way if you understand that these experiences sometimes leave wounds that are difficult to heal. The art is to learn how to deal with these wounds.

GIVE YOURSELF A TRANSIT ZONE

Letting go of the past does not mean that you will automatically feel comfortable in the new situation in which you find yourself. Most people need a period of reflection and adjustment between what was and what will be. Former Harvard professor William Bridges called this the 'neutral zone'. The length of time that people need to come to terms with the new situation will vary, depending on their personality and the circumstances.

Give yourself a transit period for every new and important event in your life.

It's like having a burnt pan you want to clean: you can only do it if you let it soak for a while. This is the transit zone. How long does it last? 'As long as it takes' is the only correct answer. Sometimes you need to leave the pan in water for minutes; sometimes for hours, even longer. But however long it takes, the important thing is to soak the pan and not leave it standing burnt on the stove. Because if you do, it will be difficult to clean it later on – perhaps even impossible. Your once shiny pan will be lost forever.

Transit zones are an essential part of every change process. It would have been perfectly normal for Steven to have taken things easy in the months after his heart attack (although this can't last forever). Give yourself a transition period for every new and important event in your life: after an illness or operation, after a dismissal or promotion, after the birth of your first child, after a divorce, after moving house… In short, let yourself have a good soak. Allow yourself time to digest things, flush – and then move on.

Coach yourself!

Be a fly on the wall and play through the film of your life. What have been the milestones?
What can you learn from writing down your personal story?
What do you need to let go of in the past?
Did you already let go or are you still in the transit zone? How long has this 'soaking process' already taken?
Do you still sometimes shed tears over past sorrows? When?
Write down the insights that you will later include in your identity card.

....

....

....

....

....

....

....

....

....

2. FIND YOUR PASSION

Do you sometimes look admiringly at people who are so full of confidence, so intense about life, so dynamic in everything they do, that they almost seem to glow with their passion? Well, you too can glow with that same passion. There are lots of techniques to help you. Consciously. But you have to be prepared (amongst other things) to trust your unconsciousness. In the following chapter we will see how you can search with courage for your true core. But before we can start, we first need to run through a number of concepts that often get confused.

First, our objectives. Everyone sets objectives: 'I want to lose five kilos before the end of February', 'I want to move house by the end of the year', 'I want to get that promotion before the summer holidays'. But to get to the core of who you are, we need to go much deeper than the simple setting of objectives. Because objectives are something superficial. They stay on the surface. They won't give us passion.

Second, our drivers. These are the things that excite us: for some people, it might be writing; for others it might be singing; it might even be the idea of setting up your own company. This is the core of 'I am'. Before you can fill in your identity card, you need to identify your drivers.

Third, our dream. Many people have a dream, although it often seems a long way off. But if you know what your drivers are and if they match your dream, then that dream suddenly gets closer and closer. Just visualize it!

Finally, passion. This is difficult to describe in rational terms. If you have achieved your dream and it matches the authentic you – who you are and what you want – then you will feel passion. It is an inexhaustible source of energy that will truly make you glow.

FIND YOUR FUEL

This is where the search starts for the things that really motivate you

 Note to the director

In the previous chapter we asked you to look back at your life so far. Starting here and now, we are going to look forward, searching for your fuel, for the things that excite you. In short, your drivers.

 Agnes runs a flourishing flower business. At first, she wanted to do this on her own, but because of her enormous success she later needed to take on six employees to help her. When she sits in front of me in our coaching practice, I can immediately see the stress in her face. The cost of paying her staff and the uncertainty of her market add up to a huge amount of financial pressure. During our two-hour session, Agnes manages to relax a little, but at the end of the session she says that she feels trapped in the hectic ratrace of her own life.

Many people will recognize this story. In the past, we have all had dreams, whether they were great or small. And we all probably tried to realize them, in one way or another. But the pressure of modern life makes it so easy to lose sight of what is essential, the core of our dream. As a result, it is crucial to stop and remind yourself each day of the original reasons why you do what you do. When we asked Agnes to do this, she began to talk enthusiastically about when she was little: the way she picked bunches of wild flowers on family outings and how later nothing made her happier than making a bouquet. Working with flowers made her feel calm and relaxed.

So where are the flowers in Agnes' life now? Her daily task has been reduced to managing her personnel, keeping a sharp eye on the books, haggling with suppliers…

 I see Agnes again a month later. She has taken a serious look at her life and what she does. She now makes sure

that she is working with flowers for at least three hours a day. She no longer does the bookkeeping and her staff now deal with the suppliers under her strict instructions. She tells them exactly which flowers to buy and has sent them all on a course to learn purchasing techniques. Agnes is once again surrounded by flowers. And she glows with pleasure!

SEARCHING FOR YOUR DRIVERS

Perhaps circumstances have caused you to lose sight of your dream, to lose contact with your real drivers. Perhaps your daily life is taking too much out of you, consuming your energy and your passion.

Maybe you think your story is not so different from Agnes'? If so, you need to go in search of the daily fuel that can make you happy. Dare to question yourself and your life, dare to return to the things that make your heart beat faster; identify the changes that will allow you to live your life 100% to the full.

In the previous chapter, we asked you to throw your ballast overboard and only keep the most important stones in your rucksack. Many of these stones will be 'your drivers'. As soon as you know what they are, you will find the energy to live with full commitment and satisfaction in the here and now.

In coaching terms, we call this your identity. What do you stand for? What makes you tick? It can be many different things. Some people are driven by new challenges. For them, risk and adventure are essential. Routine drives them crazy and so they always need to make new plans. For other people, caring for others might be the most important thing. Whatever drives you, you need to discover what it is. It is often enough to think back to your childhood years. Were you a Tarzan who loved climbing in trees? Or a Charlie Chaplin who skipped through life and enjoyed making people laugh? Or did you always have your nose in a book, trying to understand how the world works? There is a good chance that in your work today you will find things that have typified you since you were a child.

Ask yourself what makes your heart beat faster, what makes you happy, what gives you energy.

Ask yourself what makes your heart beat faster, what makes you happy, what gives you energy. Like Agnes', remember that your life is continually evolving, so that it is a good idea to check regularly that you are being true to your drivers. If you really take the time to look closely at your talents and dreams, you will increase your chances of living a happy life.

Do it now. You won't regret it.

We know that it is often easier said than done to identify and define your drivers in this way. So in the next chapters we will look at a few techniques that can help you on your way.

 Coach yourself!

Do you know the important drivers in your life?
What are they?
What can you learn about your drivers if you look back on your childhood years?
What really makes your heart beat faster?
What do you think is truly worthwhile?
How much time do you waste each day doing things you really don't want to do?
What used to make you happy?
Do you still find that in your life today?
What is your daily fuel?
Write down the insights that you will later include in your identity card.

....

....

....

WITH COURAGE TO THE CORE
Gaining insight into your core and what is stopping you from finding it can be deeply confrontational

Note to the director
In this and the following chapters, we will zoom in on a number of techniques that will help you to find your core. Some of these methods will be rational, others intuitive. We will begin here with the most challenging one: the labyrinth, a pattern that has been used in different cultures and different places for important rituals in life.

I have already had a number of coaching sessions with Lisa. Lisa is a rational business woman who runs a successful company. We have already analyzed several interesting subjects, but I still have the feeling that we have not yet got to the core of the matter, to the things that really count. 'Time for a non-rational approach,' I think to myself. I explain my plan to Lisa and lead her out to the labyrinth in the garden of our practice. I ask her to see the labyrinth as a metaphor for her path through life and tell her to go to its core and then come back again. 'Try not to think too much.' Lisa steps hesitantly into the labyrinth and walks steadily to its centre. From time to time she slows down, before moving on again at the same pace. Just before she reaches the centre she hesitates. She turns around and walks back the way she came. Once she arrives at my side, I immediately send her back into the labyrinth. 'And this time I want you to go all the way to the core.' Once again, she follows the path to the centre, but much more timidly, her head and shoulders pointing down. She maintains this posture, even when she has reached the centre, and then walks slowly back to where I am standing. I send her back into the labyrinth for a third time. 'And now I want you to walk with your head and shoulders erect.'
She does what I ask, and as soon as she reaches the centre of the labyrinth the tears are rolling down her cheeks.

The labyrinth is a way to get to the core of our being, because it goes beyond rational thinking.

The labyrinth is a way to get to the core of our being, because it goes beyond rational thinking. It is an ancient pattern that has been used in many different cultures all over the world. They all came into existence independently of each other and in many different variants. But wherever they developed, they were soon connected with important life rituals: the transition from puberty to adulthood, supplications for a good harvest, ceremonies to increase female fertility… And they all made use of the same principle: once you enter the labyrinth and follow its path, it will always lead you to the core.

This is different from a maze, where there are different routes to the centre and some of the paths are blocked. This means that you have to use your reason to find the right way. Mazes became popular during the Renaissance. Initially, they were intended to stimulate rational thinking, and later they often became a decorative form of outdoor entertainment.

The labyrinth goes much further than that. It challenges all of our brains: not only our reason, but also our heart and our guts, our gut feeling. In the latter we can best discover our core. They are a collection of all our experiences, impressions, feelings and sensory observations from childhood onwards, from the moment when we first saw the light of day. Taken together, all these things form our intuition. They show us the best thing to do, warn us when we need to be careful, tell us what makes us tick.

When Lisa entered the labyrinth, she was quite literally afraid to go to the core of her being. Somewhere along the path, there was 'something' that held her back. Deep down, we often know what our core is and what stops us from getting there. There can be many different reasons: too much focus on 'caring' for others, so that we forget to take care of ourselves; too much urgency to earn money, so that we actually forget to enjoy life; too much concentration on sources of 'instant' pleasure, which bring us very little satisfaction in the long term; too much fear of stepping forward into an uncertain future, so that we simply stay where we are, going nowhere. We work and work and work, but all this effort is often far removed from our convictions, our values, our norms...

The labyrinth challenges all of our brains: not only our reason, but also our heart and our guts, our gut feeling.

Gaining insight into your core – what it is and what prevents you from getting there – can be deeply confrontational. Because it may lead to the realization that you have already missed so many chances and lost so much time. But as soon as you find the courage to go to your core, once you throw off your unnecessary protective shell, you will notice that things quickly begin to fall back into place. You will once again become the director of your own life, acting and behaving as you truly are.

If you have an open mind, the labyrinth is an effective way to discover your core – although the initial threshold, as Lisa discovered, can be high. You need to be prepared for it, you need to have courage. You must be willing to surrender yourself to 'not knowing'. It is impossible to formulate a rational answer to explain how the labyrinth leads us to our core. All we can say is that experience shows that it works for many people. Even so, the need to surrender to the 'unknown' can often be hard. We are so used to consciously initiating action and doing things that we no longer know what it means just to 'be'. This helps to explain the huge present-day popularity of mindfulness, meditation, yoga, etc.

We no longer know what it means to just 'be'.

In essence, these techniques are easy to learn. All it requires is for you to set your judgements aside.

Coach yourself!

What do you need before you have the courage to go to your core?
If you have ever walked in a labyrinth, what kind of feeling did it give you? (If you have never done it, you should really give it a try.)
When were you last in a maze?
What feeling did that give you?
What do you need to let go of your rational thinking?
Write down the insights that you will later include in your identity card.

....

....

....

....

....

....

....

....

....

THE SCRIPT OF YOUR LIFE

There are different ways to discover your drivers, which go far beyond your simple objectives

Note to the director
In this chapter, you will read about a number of concrete methods that will help you to find the way to your core. What many of these methods have in common is the way they set our rational thinking aside, just like the labyrinth. You can't find your core by using your head alone.

There are different ways to search for our true drivers. In exceptional cases, you may be able to discover them by pure intuition, but normally this will require:
1. Courage
2. Time
3. Energy
4. A number of tools to help you

As we mentioned in the introduction, we can't give you courage: you must find that for yourself. What we *can* do is make you aware that you will also need lots of time and energy. There are also various tools that can help you to find the way to your core.

Charles takes his coaching book and reads out what he wrote: 'I want to be a successful leader by the time I am forty.'
'What does that mean for you, being a "successful leader"?' I ask him.
'Having a team that is 100% behind me, achieving greater productivity and earning lots of money.'

Objectives are important ambitions that we strive to achieve and can tick off as soon as we reach them. Drivers are something deep down inside us.

We have already discussed the difference between objectives and drivers. Objectives are important ambitions that we strive to achieve and can tick off as soon as we reach them. Drivers are something deep down inside us. In the above example, Charles is not talking about his drivers, but about the objectives he has set for himself. There are different ways to discover what motives lay behind those objectives. Rational ways, but also less rational ways. In Charles' case, we chose one of the less rational ways: we went for a walk with him on Kalmthout Moors, near our coaching practice.

Charles looks at me suspiciously. 'What has going for a walk got to do with coaching?'
'I want you to get completely away from a working environment,' I reply.
'Anything you say, coach,' he laughs.
Ten minutes later we are out on the moor.
We start walking at a steady tempo and I begin asking him questions. Sometimes we fall quiet, just looking at the landscape and listening to the sounds of nature. Then we carry on walking at the same pace. When I sense that the silence is no longer uncomfortable, I ask: 'What's going through your head right now?'
'I was thinking about your question and what it means to be a successful leader.' 'And?'
Now he is walking more slowly and looks at me thoughtfully: 'It's not as simple as I thought,' he says. 'I've got a feeling that there's more to it than the things I mentioned, but I don't know what.'

If, by the time he is forty, Charles has a number of people working for him, has increased productivity and is earning more money, then he will have reached his objectives. However, there is a good chance that he will still feel empty inside. It is important that he digs deeper to find out more about his real drivers. It is only when objectives are linked to drivers that they become truly powerful.

'NATURAL' INSPIRATION

Nature is a great source of inspiration. We took Charles up onto the Kalmthout Moor for a reason. In a 'natural' setting you are more likely to discover the things that are 'natural' to you. If you don't believe us, just give it a try. Put on your walking shoes and set off into the wild, preferably alone. Look at the things you meet along the way – literally. It might be a strangely formed branch that catches your attention or a brightly coloured mushroom. Perhaps you suddenly hear the call of a bird or notice how the rays of the sun filter through the leaves of the trees. What do all these things mean for you? Ask yourself what is really important. And when you are in the right mood (perhaps after several walks), ask yourself the key question: 'If I look back at the end of my life at who I was, who would I like to see?'

This is an example of a deep identity question that takes time, courage and energy to answer.

QUESTIONS, QUESTIONS AND MORE QUESTIONS

Another more rational method to discover your core is by repeated self-questioning.

Let's start with the example of Charles, which began with:
'As a successful leader I will have a team that is 100% behind me, will increase productivity and will be earning lots of money.'
'So what does that bring you, once you have reached your objectives?'
'More prestige.'
'And once you have prestige, what will that give you?'
'Greater respect from others.'
'And what will that respect give you?'
'It will make me feel better about who I am.'
'And once you feel better, where will that take you?'
'It will give me the courage to do the things I really want to do, but never dared in the past.'
'And if you dare to do those things, what will that mean?'
'That I will finally have more time to play my saxophone.'
'And after all those hours practicing your sax, where will that lead you?'
'Then I will start up our old band again, so there will be music in my life again.'

You only stop this exercise when you reach the point where you can get no further. The final answer often comes after the fifth or sixth question. If you go on for much longer, you will find your thoughts going around in circles, repeating the same answers over and over. It is usually pretty clear when you have arrived at your core, because you will feel a surge of new energy coursing through your veins.

When people ask themselves the question 'What is important for me?', the answers can be very different. We hear things like 'living in a green environment', or 'having a challenging job', or 'finding a better balance between my work and my family'. But whatever the answer, you need to keep on questioning: 'What would living in a green environment give to you?' 'I would feel more at ease.' 'And how would that change things?' 'I would have more space to breathe and wouldn't feel trapped inside four walls, like I do in the office.' 'And what would that space give you?' 'Freedom! Freedom to live my own life.'

THE IDENTITY MATRIX

The identity matrix, developed by Robert Dilts, is an excellent and intense way to discover your core. The exercise consists of answering six fundamental questions that determine your identity.

Find a place where you won't be disturbed and can relax. Make sure you are sitting or standing comfortably and have a pen and paper with you. Draw the following table on a blank paper.

1	3	5
2	4	6

Write down your answers to the questions below, starting in the top left hand corner (1), then in the bottom left (2), then in the middle top (3), then in the middle bottom (4), then in the top right (5) and finally in the bottom right (6).

Please don't look at the table that has already been filled in on the following page.

Don't think too much about the answers, but write down the first thing that comes into your head. It can be a feeling, a profession, an animal, even a noise. It doesn't matter. This is all about you and nobody will ever see your answers, unless you want to share them.

Here are the six questions:
- » What would you like to be and never will be? (box 1)
- » What do you not want to be and never will be? (box 2)
- » What would you like to be and might possibly become? (box 3)
- » What do you not want to be and might possibly become? (box 4)
- » What would you like to be and always will be? (box 5)
- » What do you not want to be and always will be? (box 6)

When you have finished, take a look at your answers and let them sink in.

Your answers are essential parts of your identity. We will now look at what these answers indicate.

Box 1: The first answer is your limitation, the part of your identity you are constantly striving to achieve but will never reach.

Box 2: The second answer is your boundary, the point beyond which you will never cross.

Box 3: The third answer is your potential. This is well within your reach and is therefore a good driver to make your objectives more concrete and better suited to who you are.

Box 4: This answer shows your weak points or the traps into which you might fall. Be careful to avoid these.

Box 5: This answer is your deep core. This is what you stand for. This is what makes you you. This is what you want to cherish and to show more and more to other people.

Box 6: This is your shadow. You cannot escape this, but it is important to speak or write its name, so that you are aware of its existence and can learn to live with it.

Limitation	Potential	Deep core
Boundary	Weakness	Shadow

 Stella's identity matrix

As free as a bird	A strong woman leading her own company	Alice in Wonderland
A criminal	Passivity: staying where I am because I am afraid to move	Little Miss Stressy

Stella looks at her answers. 'What do you think?' I ask her.
'I'm trying to see the connections,' she says.
'What does Alice in Wonderland mean for you?'
'I am at my best if I can marvel at things without judging them. Then I can be very creative and do a lot.'
'And how can Alice in Wonderland help you to be a strong woman who runs her own company?'
'Oh, that would help me tremendously.' The energy level in Stella's voice hits the roof. She starts talking at a hundred miles an hour. We look for the connections between her answers. Stella realizes that Little Miss Stressy is too prominent in her current job. She explains how one day she passively does nothing, followed the next day by trying to do far too much all at the same

time, so that she ends up running around like a headless chicken. I notice that her energy level begins to drop when she talks about her work, but rises again when she talks about the creative projects she has taken part in during her life. Slowly but surely, Stella understands that Alice in Wonderland will be harder and harder to find, if she stays in her current job.

Our identity is not made up of exclusively good things. The top row of boxes in the matrix show the positive sides of our personality, while the bottom three boxes show the less positive aspects. But it is important not to ignore these negative traits, because the more you are aware of them, the more you will want – and be able – to concentrate on the core of your potential.

That's also how it was for Alice, the main character in the famous (children's) book *Alice in Wonderland* (1865) by the English writer and mathematician Lewis Carroll. One day, Alice follows a talking white rabbit down its hole. She falls through the bottom of this hole and finds herself in Wonderland, where she meets all kind of weird and wonderful beings and has dozens of bizarre experiences. At one point, she finds herself in a house where there is a drink that makes her grow to such a huge size that she gets stuck inside the house. Alice now has two options: she can do nothing and simply moan about her bad luck or else she can try to find another drink that will make her smaller again, so that she can carry on with her adventures. And we all know which option she chose...

We all need to keep moving forward in life; after all, we only get one shot at it. How you live that life is something that you – and you alone – can decide. You can let yourself be inhibited by limiting thoughts or else, like Alice, you can look at all the wonders around you and embrace them to the full.

BUY YOURSELF A DIARY

If you haven't got a diary or if you haven't written anything in it for years, now is the moment to buy a new one or dust off the old one. Of course, you can always keep an electronic diary on your computer, but we advise to use a paper version. Take the time to think some more about the things that are important to you. Write words, make drawings, use photos, listen to inspiring music, draw tables... It doesn't matter as long as you are focusing on the process. The better you know who you really are and what makes you tick, the richer your life will become. Your drivers will then form the basis for your objectives and actions. You were born to be the director of your own life – so make sure you take matters into your own hands and find the energy to do it well.

Coach yourself!

How high is your energy level (on a scale of 0 to 10)?
How can you increase this level, if necessary?
In which setting can you think best about your drivers?
Which tools can you best use and who can help you with this?
What is your preferred tool? And how can you leave your comfort zone to try out a new tool that is perhaps less evident?
What are your objectives and how are they linked to your drivers?
Write down the insights that you will later include in your identity card.

....

....

....

....

LIVE YOUR DREAM

Live your dream by turning your drivers into objectives

 Note to the director
In the last chapter, we learned different techniques to discover your core. In this chapter, we are going to learn how to dream. The more concretely you can envisage your dream, the more real it will become, just like those dreams at night that which seem so real that you wake up with a start. In the following pages we will see how you can use your dreams to help turn your drivers into objectives.

Think about the dreams you have at night.

When you dream at night, you can sometimes remember details so clearly that they leave nothing to the imagination. But dreams are not always full of sweetness and light. Dreams can sometimes be tense, difficult or even frightening.

When we ask our coachees about their dream life, we frequently hear beautiful stories: how they will achieve success, what that would mean for them, how it would change their life for the better... Truly amazing! But the reality is often different. No matter how much people want to make their dreams come true, it doesn't always work – or at least not in the way they imagined it. Sadly, this happens far more often than you might think...

'SEE' YOUR DREAM

Lots of things have been written about the power of visualization. Sports coach Tim Gallwey, one of the 'inventors' of coaching (which largely had its origins in the sporting world) described it as follows: 'The opponent in your head is much bigger than the one on the other side of the net.' If you can get rid of the

If you can get rid of the opponent in your head and can 'see' your success, you have much more chance of actually becoming successful.

opponent in your head and can 'see' your success, you have much more chance of actually becoming successful!

We once had a powerful experience of this form of visualization. At the press conference for the launch of our first book, *Be who you really want to be*, a number of people from China were present. Just when the publisher was ready to present our book, we saw them standing in the corner. We looked at each other and later on asked: 'Were you thinking what I was thinking?' And yes, in our mind's eye we both 'saw' our book being printed and distributed in China. We not only hoped that this would happen, but both of us really started to believe it. We went in search of a Chinese translator and soon found one. True, we first needed to have the book translated into English, so we didn't make things easy for ourselves. But the Chinese translator was able to point us in the direction of a Chinese publisher and the rest – as they say – is history. The book was published in Mandarin by the Nanfang Daily Press.

What can we learn from this? Visualization works. But you really need to believe in it and must make the necessary effort. If you just adopt a 'wait-and-see' attitude, nothing is ever going to happen.

Christine leads a happy life. She has a part-time office job, two wonderful kids and an equally wonderful husband. Even so, for the last ten years she has been planning to do 'something different', something independent that will allow her to express her true self and use her talents to the full. 'But I just never seem to get around to finding the new challenge I'm looking for,' she says with a sigh.
It is not the first time I have heard her complain about this. 'Christine, describe to me exactly what you want. Tell me your dream story.'
Christine drifts away into thought. I give her all the time she needs. And then she starts talking, hesitantly at first, but soon with ever increasing enthusiasm. I ask her for more details and this serves to increase the thrill of the moment for her. She is glowing.
When she has finished her story, I ask her to step back into that success moment. I ask her what she saw and

how she felt. In particular, I ask her if she can remember how her voice sounded and what happened with the people around her. How much energy did she feel? When Christine is fully ready, I ask her to take a mental photograph of the best possible state of success. We repeat this a number of times in later sessions and I task her to do the same at home and at work, several times a day over a long period.

This is not the only way to prompt her into action, but it will certainly help.

 Take a blank sheet of paper and some coloured pencils. Draw on the paper the elements in your life (it doesn't matter how many) that get you excited. But you can only use your left hand (or your right hand if you are left-handed)! Do it now, before you read any further.

When you have finished, write down next to the elements what they represent.

Keep the drawing and look at it regularly. Check that all the elements are still sufficiently present in your life. If they aren't, do something about it.

The reason why we asked you to do this with your non-dominant hand is that this forces you to use the right side of your brain. This is where your creative brain – your intuition – is situated. In short, everything that you can't immediately put into words. Sometimes it is necessary to tap into your intuition if you want to know what really drives you.

> *Sometimes it is necessary to tap in to your intuition, if you want to know what really drives you.*

FEEL, HEAR, SMELL

Visualization is just a small part of the story. We also have other senses to help us, although we probably don't use them enough.

If you dream about finding a job in France, listen to the French news. If you dream of having a house with a beautiful garden, put a fragrant rose next to your computer. If you want to do more sport and know that music inspires you, play that song that always gets you dancing on your chair.

This is why we don't simply talk about the power of visualization. You also need to remember the power of hearing, feeling and smelling, if you want to make your dream come true.

 Here is a fun tip to help you on your way.
When you see your dream, or hear it, or experience it, ask yourself the following related questions.
If you can answer these questions, you will have a detailed dream image to work with towards the future. If you can't give all the answers, your dream image is still not clear enough.

Think about your dream.
(For example, I want to run a bed and breakfast).

Now ask the following questions:

Where?
(In Tuscany.)

What?
(A farm with six or so bedrooms, a swimming pool, some sheep, chickens and a biological vegetable garden.)

When?
(No later than the end of next year.)

How?
(I'm going to study the sector, to learn what works and what doesn't, and I'm going to spend the summer in Italy searching for inspirational examples.)

Who with?
(My partner, who shares the same dream.)

What can I hear?
(I can hear a cockerel, the crickets, the bleating of sheep, people having breakfast outside, children playing.)

What can I see?
(A broad landscape, soft colours, vineyards, beautiful and authentic rooms.)

What do I feel?
(Intense happiness, peace, satisfaction.)

Your image will be much clearer after you have answered these questions.

People process information visually (seeing), aurally (hearing) or kinaesthetically (feeling). Perhaps you already know which of these three channels works best in your case. Or perhaps you don't. If not, ask yourself the following question: if you think of something you want to achieve, do you see a detailed and life-like image in your head? Or do you first hear voices and noises? Or perhaps you see moving images in your thoughts: can you feel the emotions they convey?

It sounds more difficult than it really is. Thankfully, there is a simple way to find out which channel suits you best.

An example:
I am sitting in a team meeting and I see the colours of the presentation and notice that the right-hand column is not properly aligned (seeing, visual).
I am sitting in a team meeting and I hear the buzz of the air-conditioning and the constant clicking of my neighbour's pen (hearing, aural).
I am sitting in a team meeting and I feel the cool breeze through the open window (feeling, kinaesthetic)

Don't forget that everyone can usually make use of all three channels, but one will be better developed than the others. This is sometimes connected with the person's job. For example, a fashion designed will have less need of the aural channel, since he can design new clothes in complete silence. In contrast, for a pianist the aural channel will be by far the strongest of the three. When you watch a concert pianist, you can often see him playing with eyes closed: the visual channel is (relatively) unimportant. It's different again for a ballet dancer, where the kinaesthetic channel – the sense of feeling – is best developed. So which one is most important for you?

 Dirk enters my office enthusiastically. With a big smile on his face, he tells me that he has done his homework. Dirk works in an advertising office and told me during a previous session that he would be able to win an important customer if his trial presentation for the launch of a new product is a success. This presentation is planned to take place in three weeks time for a varied audience: the financiers of the project, the people who will develop the video clip and Dirk's own bosses. During our last session, we spoke about the importance of addressing his public through the three channels, so that he could attract the attention of everyone present. The idea is to use this session as practice for the real presentation.

Dirk has indeed done his homework, preparing everything down to the smallest detail. First of all, he shows me a very clear video presentation. This includes figures for the profit margin of the new product, so that everyone can see what his proposal involves. And while he is talking, Dirk adjusts his voice to match the images on the screen. Finally, he hands me a small towel that has been washed with the new product. This way, I can feel and smell its quality.

I am carried away by his presentation. 'Success guaranteed,' I tell him.

A MEANINGFUL CHOICE OF WORDS

Three weeks later, Dirk's presentation was indeed a great success. During the practice session, we also talked about the importance of choosing and using words in the right way. Your choice of words shows which channels you are using to address the other person(s). Similarly, you can discover from others which channel they prefer from the way they talk to you.

If you want to make your dream seem real, experience it with all your senses.

Someone who is primarily visual will use words like sight, clear, dark, blurry, yellow, dazzling, black-and-white, eye-catching, clarify, etc. An aural person is more likely to use terms such as conversation, deaf, muted, mumbling, whistling, hoarse, shouting, laugh, hear, etc. Words like taste, feel, flavour, melted, stress, fear, pleasure, smell, aroma, fragrance, sultry, pain and happy mean that you are probably talking to someone who prefers the kinaesthetic channel.

In short, if you want to make your dream seem real, you need to experience it with all your senses. And because it helps to persuade others to believe in and support your dream, always use all three channels to convince them of its feasibility and power.

 Coach yourself!

Have you ever looked in detail at your dream life? Answer your dream image questions: where, what, when, how and with whom?
What do I see, hear and feel? Which channel do you prefer for processing information?
Can you give examples of people who process information in a way that is different from yours? Who?
How can your dreams help to transform your drivers into concrete objectives?
Write down the insights that you will later include in your identity card.

....

....

DRENCH YOUR FILM WITH PASSION
Deal consciously with the things you really want

Note to the director
If your three brains – your heart, your gut and your head – all coincide, you will be able to make the film of your life into a real blockbuster. In this next chapter, you can read how.

Micheline is sitting in front of me and she is beaming. She has just been nominated as one of the three finalists for the Womed Awards. We look at the speech that she will give to the award committee. I listen in fascination to the text she reads out to me. Her message encapsulates everything she said to me during our coaching sessions in recent months. She talks about the start of her company and how it has grown to become a successful business. She talks about the importance of female entrepreneurship and the connection between the inner and outer worlds. She talks about her commitment towards her staff and how she continues to learn from them, day after day… Afterwards, she says: 'It's easy when I read it to you, because with you I can say it from the heart. But I'm not sure I can do that when I need to read it to the audience tonight.'
'Of course you can,' I tell her. 'When you are full of passion, like you are, you always speak from the heart. Nothing can stop you.' She looks at me and we laugh. I can feel her energy bubbling away inside her.

The speech was a big success.

Passion makes you glow within. It is something deep inside you, an inexhaustible source of energy that helps you to keep going. If you know how to use that source properly, other people around you will soon notice. Perhaps you know someone like that? Someone who not only manages to get everything done, but gets it done well. Someone who never appears to experience any difficulties and is always bursting with vitality. There are lots of well-known public figures like this: think of Elon Musk (Tesla) in the business world or Beyoncé in show biz.

Passion is the superlative of enthusiasm. Some people are enthusiastic by nature or find their enthusiasm by being motivated by others. But nobody can give you passion. It is part of your nature. That's why, when we talk about passion, we often speak of our 'gut feeling': it comes from the very core of our being. And the term 'gut feeling' actually means much more than you might think at first glance.

COMBINING YOUR THREE BRAINS = PASSION

We have already mentioned your three different types of brains. During the last ten years, much research has been carried out on this subject. In the past, we were much too concerned with the use of our head brain. Thankfully, our other brains are steadily becoming the object of our attention as well. These other brains were much more important in ancient times, but in our modern world they have largely been forgotten. However, science has now shown that each of the three brains has its own neural network:

If you go through life with passion, you are not only thinking with your head. Passionate people use all three brains, working together in harmony.

» The 'gut' brain is the core of our identity and represents our self-preservation and our drivers.
» The 'heart' brain is the centre of our emotions, our values and everything connected with our relationships.
» The 'head' brain is our centre of thought and the meaning we give to things.

Did you know that the gut brain is the first to be developed in a human embryo, followed by the heart brain and finally by the head brain? The nine months of pregnancy are therefore a microcosm of the evolution of mankind.

If you go through life with passion, you are not only thinking with your head. Passionate people use all three brains, working together in harmony.

ACTIVATE YOUR PASSION

People who are passionate about something achieve better results.

If you have done your 'homework' properly, you should already know from the previous chapters what is important to you. You will have discovered your 'gut feeling' and listened to what your heart has to tell you. But when we speak of passion, we mean that all three brains are working closely together. The trick is to make the feeling of passion your own, by activating your enthusiasm for the things you consider important.

Ask yourself if you are passionate about your job, your hobbies, your sport. People who are enthusiastic about these things are usually successful in what they do. If you go through life with passion, you jump out of bed each morning and are immediately ready to start the day. You feel the energy coursing through your body and you have a clear idea of what you want to do.

Your passion is often linked to major objectives and big dreams, but can just as easily involve small, everyday tasks.

Your passion is often linked to major objectives and big dreams, but can just as easily involve small, everyday tasks.

 Here is an exercise that can help you to activate your passion. Think of something you have to do in the next few days. 'But what something?' I hear you ask. This is where the exercise begins.

First listen to your heart, because your heart knows what is most important. Breathe calmly in and out three or four times. Now focus on your heart and continue breathing calmly. Ask yourself the following question: What is my most important task in the days ahead?

For example:
You want to make a short information film about your company, which is specialized in computer applications. Too many people keep on asking you the same questions about practical problems.

What does your heart tell you?
If I make this film and upload it online, where it can be viewed for free, I will be able to help a lot of people. It will give them the opportunity to watch the film as often as they like and it would also save me a lot of time. This would make it possible to work more on our applications, which are our real added value. After all, that's the reason why I started the company in the first place.

As soon as you know which important task you have chosen and have felt the emotion related to it, you now need to focus on your gut, because it is your gut feeling that jogs you into action. Continue to breathe calmly. What does your gut feeling tell you about your idea to make an information film? For example, I want to have enough energy to make the film. Stay with this gut feeling for a few moments and listen to what your gut says about putting your idea into action.

If I am going to do it, I want to do it well. The film needs to radiate our company values, yet still be easy and simple to follow, so that everyone can get something from it.

Only now are you ready to move on to your head brain, because your head gives meaning to what you have already learned from the other two brains. Using your head, you can make concrete plans.

For example:
I will start tomorrow by writing the scenarios. I will also clear a space in one of our offices with enough light and good acoustics, where we can do the filming. By the end of next week it will be ready and I will be able to upload it onto the web. I will announce the idea in a newsletter and on social media, so that people other than my customers can view it.

By listening to your three brains, your tasks not only become jobs to be ticked off your 'to do' list when completed, but are also actions that are drenched in your energy and passion.

SHARED PASSION?

Passion is not exclusive to individuals. Passions can be shared. For example, colleagues can be passionate about the same project. When this happens, they find themselves in the same 'flow', which allows them to move mountains. If you are the leader of such a team, you are a very lucky person.

> I am coaching a team who are drawing up their mission statement for Europe. They are in the garden, working in two groups on the same theme. After half an hour, I call them back inside.
> Each group puts forward its draft of the mission statement. The two missions have many similarities. My heart beats faster: the energy levels seem good. I facilitate the discussion and we soon come to a joint text that incorporates all the different views.

The fact that these two groups, working separately, drew up very similar mission statements is meaningful. It implies that they share the same culture and that their noses are all pointing in the same direction. But putting down a mission on paper is only the beginning. The real work starts now. They will need to enthuse their staff to work together with them to accomplish the mission. This will only happen if they act as 'ambassadors' for the mission, communicating their passion to others and energizing them to concerted action.

> I write out the new mission statement on a flip chart. After everyone has taken a seat, I go and stand in front of them, with the mission in my hand. I can feel the importance of this work, the sense of responsibility it embodies. I look at each person in the room, one by one. 'This is your mission for Europe.' My voice is warm and I speak slowly and thoughtfully. 'This is more than just words on paper. You need to make this mission your own. You need to feel what the words mean for each of you. Only then will you be able to carry this message as a team to the rest of your organization. And believe me, your other colleagues will be able to feel your passion.'

> Twelve pairs of eyes look at me, full of enthusiasm and I can feel the energy flooding through my body.

Where is your passion right now? In one of the earlier chapters, we asked you to think about the things that are most important to you; so that you could identify your dreams and drivers, and discover where you really want to go. Now it is time to pause and reflect. If you think about your dreams and drivers, do you do this with passion? Can you feel it in your heart and gut? We would like you to think again about why you do what you do and about the things that make you happy today.

When you fill your life with passion, the days simply fly by. You are able to do more in less time. You make better decisions. You attract others to you like a magnet, because of your positive aura. They want to be associated with you and your success. So who is the 'real' you and what aura do you want to radiate?

 Coach yourself!

How do you find your own vibrant passion?
Do you listen to your three brains? What do they tell you?
Do you also put your passion into the small things in life? How?
How will you make sure to fill in your identity card with passion?
Make sure you notice what you experience while filling it in.
What more can you do to activate your passion?
Write down the insights that you will later include in your identity card.

....

....

....

3. TAKE GOOD CARE OF YOURSELF

In the previous section about 'I am', you went in search of your identity, your passion. But that is not enough. Your real you, your true identity, also needs fuel and oxygen to function properly. And that means you need to take good care of that 'I am'. Because if you don't, you will lose control and no longer be the director of your own film.

Nowadays, we are mainly preoccupied with what's in our head, but the body is just as important. Body and mind form a single whole; one cannot function without the other. Today, this is described as the biopsychosocial model. In other words, we are beings in which the biological (body), the psychological (mind) and the social (interaction) are all combined.

For this reason, in the following chapters we will look more closely at the ways in which you can take good care of yourself, both physically and mentally.

WALK YOUR BODY
A chapter full of attention for your body

 Note to the director
Take good care of yourself! Because you only have one body, which is your home for the rest of your days, it is plain common sense to make sure that you look after it properly. You need to feed it, nurture it and treat it with love. You know you can't exchange it for another, so make the best of what you've got. Treat it well and it will last you your whole life long.

I open the door and look into a sweaty but smiling face. It is time for Kate's coaching session and she is clearly full of energy. Dressed in her sports clothes, she almost sprints into my office.
'I cycled here. Great fun! And it makes me feel super happy.'
It also makes me happy to see a very different Kate from the one I saw a few months ago, when we started our coaching. From a dispirited woman drained of energy she has been transformed into a lively jack-in-the-box. Kate had a very low energy level when we first met. The words burn-out, depression, and chronic fatigue syndrome were mentioned several times. To be honest, I was worried about her. Her sallow skin, her sad expression, her thin and reedy voice… They were all clear signs that everything was far from well with her. Working together with a doctor, we gradually built up Kate's resilience step by step. She was prepared to do anything, she said, as long as it gave her back her energy.

When you feel good about yourself and are in top condition, you have a healthy dose of resilience that people around you can't fail to notice. This helps you to function to the best of your ability, so that you feel even better. You are in a positive upwards spiral.

Kate now knows that her body and mind are inextricably linked to each other. She follows coaching for one and takes regular exercise for the other. She eats healthily and makes sure she gets enough rest. No marathons for Kate, but she goes for a walk every day, as well as swimming and cycling whenever she can (like today). And believe me: her body really feels the benefit of it!

YOUR BODY IN GOOD CONDITION

What happens with your body when you are in good condition? If you are in balance, the centre of gravity of your body will be somewhere around your pelvis. This gives you a supple and self-confident posture.

You will automatically walk with a more upright stance, so that your head will be pushed slightly backwards, with your chin at an angle of 90 degrees. Your muscles relax and you will be able to breathe more deeply. These deep breaths provide your body with the essential oxygen it needs.

This is the natural posture for your body.

TRY THIS OUT

Lean backwards, but gently. Try for a moment to forget the cares of the day and concentrate on your breathing. Perhaps you will notice for the first time that your breaths are shallow. Sit upright on a chair (don't slouch!). Keep your back straight, push your shoulders back and bring your chin up to an angle of 90 degrees. Can you feel the difference? Breathe in calmly through your nose until your tummy swells. Place your hand on your tummy, so that you can feel what is happening. Breathe in as deeply as you can in your pelvis.

Then breathe out through your mouth. Calmly.

Repeat this and try to focus exclusively on your breathing. Also try it standing up. Keep your back straight and your head erect.

Once you have done this several times, you will start to feel calmer. You might be a little uncertain at first, but don't let this breathing technique be influenced by your other thoughts. Just be aware that at this moment you are giving your body a wonderful present.

As usual, Lesley is late for our appointment. She seems restless, and this is not the first time. She starts telling her story while she is still crossing the room. I don't even get the chance to ask her what she wants to talk about today. While the words come pouring out, I calmly observe her. Such a good-looking woman, so stylish. Perfect make-up, trendy hair-do, elegant blue two-piece.

It has all been very carefully thought about, and that's before we even mention her shoes…

After five minutes, I have heard enough. 'Lesley, please, … stop!'

She stops mid-sentence.

'Am I doing it again?' She laughs.

'Yes, you're doing it again.' She knows what's coming next and so prepares herself.

'Lesley, let's just take a moment to breathe. Relax your muscles. Put your hands on your tummy. Breathe in… and out…'

A few minutes later, Lesley starts her story again. But this time she is much more relaxed and her voice has a rich, deep tone. This is much nicer to listen to.

A FREE PRESENT

If you are in good condition, you can breathe more easily. And thanks to good breathing, your body will develop an even better condition. Oxygen is essential and is one of the important things we get in life for free. When you are born, the very first thing you do is breathe. And when you die, you also breathe your last breath. But even though we are born with a perfect way of breathing (just look at a baby and see how round its stomach gets when it is inhaling), we lose this skill as we grow older.

Short, shallow breathing makes you restless. It's as if you are being hounded, and after a while that's the way you feel. Your words follow each other quickly; your voice gets higher and shriller. In short, you give a nervous impression. Even so, many people still see this as something positive. 'Oh, he's always so terribly busy. I'm sure he's important and must be doing very well for himself.' Really? Or is he perhaps just a stress bunny?

> *Short, shallow breathing makes you restless. You seem as though you are being hounded, and after a while that's the way you feel.*

When you regularly focus on your breathing and know how to do it, calmly and deeply, you give a very different impression to the outside world. You are convincing and easily understood. People can listen to you better, because your voice sounds more pleasant and you come across as self-assured. Everyone will think that you have everything nicely under control. Nor should you underestimate the impact it will have on yourself. If you regularly exercise this technique at quiet moments, in time your body will automatically adopt it in moments of stress. So the message is clear: take a deep breath.

REGULAR MAINTENANCE

Taking good care of your body means eating healthily, exercising sufficiently and monitoring your breathing. But it goes beyond that.

It is also about regularity, discipline and perseverance.
You can look for all kinds of reasons outside yourself to explain why you don't take care of your body, but at the end of the day you know that this makes no sense. Don't kid yourself that your body will remain in tip-top condition if you just sit around and do nothing. It won't!

If you have a dog, you probably walk it at least twice a day. Why? Because you love your dog and want it to remain fit and healthy. But how often do you walk your body? If your answer is 'never' or 'not enough', what a shame. It looks like you love your dog more than you love your body.

How is your cholesterol and blood sugar? Don't wait for your body to break down before you take it to the 'garage'...

It's just the same with your car. You have it regularly serviced to check oil, water, brakes, etc. Even if it is running well, you don't want it to break down – because you know what a pain in the neck breakdowns can be...

When was the last time you had your eyes tested? How is your cholesterol and blood sugar? Don't wait for your body to break down before you take it to the 'garage'...

Physical exercise is an important part of life – or should be. There are plenty of options. So there is no excuse for saying 'I don't like exercise'. There is something out there for everyone, even for you. And it doesn't have to be sport. Why not use the stairs instead of taking the office lift? Park your car down the road instead of in front of the door. Cycle to the bakery instead of taking a bus. Of course, joining a sports club is fine as well. And if you take up fitness or yoga, you can even do it in your own home. You don't even need to leave the house.

All that matters is that you do something, and do it with discipline and perseverance. Start off gently and find your own pace.

Lack of time is no excuse either, because then you are once again looking for reasons outside yourself to explain your own inaction. If you have a busy job, take a stroll at lunchtime. Are you driving the kids to their gym lesson? Take a walk while you wait, instead of just sitting in the car. If you are serious about taking good care of your body, you will always find a solution. When you do, you will also be giving your mind extra breathing space. And you will feel fitter, healthier and more relaxed in general.

 Coach yourself!

> You need your body your whole life long.
> In which way do you treat it lovingly?
> How often a day do you think consciously about your breathing?
> Do you know that your body is satisfied with even little efforts?
> How can you notice this?
> What excuses do you look for to avoid taking care of your body?
> How often do you walk your body?
> Write down the insights that you will later include in your identity card.

CHARGE YOUR BATTERIES – OFTEN
Search for your energy givers

 Note to the director
Self-care is the basis for a happy life. In the previous chapter, we talked about the physical aspects of self-care. In this chapter, we will be looking at ways that you can 'treat' yourself. Allow yourself some rest. Regularly charge your batteries.

You probably recharge one or more of your electronic devices every single day: your telephone, your tablet, your computer, etc. Even your electric toothbrush needs to be recharged. But do you ever have the feeling that your own batteries need recharging? You run from one meeting to the next, your partner phones to ask if you can pick something up from the supermarket, before rushing across town to collect the kids from their piano lesson. When you get home, it would be nice to settle down for a lazy evening in front of the TV, but you know that you still have three files you need to work through for your presentation tomorrow morning…

Do you feel exhausted? If so, the first question to ask is: where is your personal battery recharger?

Maybe you work as a recharger for others. You are the one who people call when their lives don't run according to plan. Colleagues come to you to pour their heart out. If your boss has a problem, you are the one he confides in. You are the shoulder for your partner to cry on. You are the one who has to fetch, carry and drive the kids, even at the most impossible moments. Not to mention your mother and the in-laws, who are always complaining that it has been 'so long' since they last saw you, even though you were there at the weekend! If you find yourself agreeing whole-heartedly with the previous sentences and you get the feeling you are in the exact same situation: it's charge-up time.

 I can see the sun shining on Camilla's face. But she doesn't seem very happy. When I ask her what subject she wants to talk about today, the first thing I hear is a sigh. 'I don't understand it. I've had a two-week holiday and I wasn't able to do a single thing. I planned to tidy up my office, finish off a few old cases, give my house a good clean. But I couldn't do any of it. I've just run out of steam…'

If this was one of those competitions where the jury rings the bell to eliminate the candidate who makes a mistake, Camilla would be hearing the bell right now. Taking leave so that you can work: it's something you hear more and more. People work, work, work, almost non-stop. The domestic and other 'to-do' lists just keep on growing, and we have an almost manic desire to tick them off as completed, even during the holiday periods, when we should be taking things a bit easier.

Taking leave so that you can work: it's something you hear of more and more. People work, work work, almost non-stop.

Today, it has almost become the new normal. But doesn't that sound wrong to you? Shouldn't we be able to arrange things better than this? The answer is self-evident but oh so difficult.

'So what you're saying, Camilla, is that during your holiday you were mainly busy catching up on your "to-do" lists?'
'Yes, I'm afraid so. I can't rest if I know there are things to do and I'm just too lazy to do them,' she says resolutely.
'Camilla, can you explain to me exactly what the word "holiday" means to you?'
'Rest, relaxation, reading, enjoyment…' This answer comes as spontaneously as her previous one. But while she is speaking, she begins to smile.
'Yes, you've got me. I can see now where things are going wrong.' Two days later, I receive a message and a photo from Camilla, lying in her back garden with a book and a cocktail. The text reads: 'Holiday = pleasure and recharging your batteries!'

YOUR RECHARGER

Working preventatively to maintain your health means that you need to recharge your batteries in time, before they run out. This is crucial, especially in a working climate where burn-out and related illnesses have become a part of our everyday existence. The fact that there is now such a thing as obligatory burn-out prevention shows that we are dealing with an epidemic that cannot be ignored.

In our western society, we are programmed – almost excessively so – on the need to perform. If you decide to do nothing for a few days, you are instantly labelled as 'lazy'. If you try to take good care of yourself, if you occasionally say 'no', if you allow yourself the pleasure of a little relaxation, you are just as quickly labelled as an egotist. And so to avoid this, we carry on working like lunatics. As a result, sooner or later one person after another is forced to stay at home for months on end because their batteries are drained.

So why not give it a try? If you feel that you are getting tired, take a little time-out to recharge your batteries. Go and lie in the garden, take an afternoon nap, flick through a magazine. It's very simple, but for many of us still so hard to achieve. We keep on hearing that nagging voice in our head: clean the car, mow the lawn, finish reading those files...

So once in a while just ignore that voice. Be aware of the thoughts you are sabotaging, and put them aside. Thoughts like: 'My wife won't like me just lying around'; 'What kind of example am I setting for the kids?'; 'My colleagues wouldn't understand'; 'What a lazy sod I really am'.

Instead, replace these thoughts with new ones, such as: 'What a difference fifteen minutes relaxation might make to the rest of the day'; 'How good would I feel if my batteries were full again'; 'Why shouldn't I allow myself a "me" moment?'; 'I'm showing my kids what self-care really means'.

The ultimate (and often most helpful) question is: 'What is the worst thing that can happen to me if I recharge my batteries?'

We repeat: give it a try.

FOCUS ON YOUR DRIVERS

We increasingly notice in our practice that people are searching for a better way of living. This search has lead to a change in awareness. We race around less and are constantly looking for the right balance. A balance we can only find in ourselves, but one that we nonetheless still seek to find in others and in the future.

You can learn to take better care of yourself by concentrating on the things that are important to you; the drivers that we talked about in previous chapters. As soon as you consciously go in search of the priorities in your life, it becomes that much easier to care for yourself properly. It is a simple fact that you get more energy when you do the things you like doing. If you realize what you really want, if you know where your true priorities lie, it is easier to follow the main thread in your life. In turn, this makes it easier to distinguish between the important and the unimportant. Once you know what your dream is, you can direct your life and the way you live towards it. Essentially, it is a question of making regular deals with yourself about what you do.

> *'No time' is the most frequent excuse, but that is really no excuse at all. We all get 24 hours a day – and that's the same for everyone in the world.*

If music is an important theme in your life, make sure you play your favourite tunes regularly. If literature is your thing, make a list of all the books you still want to read and download them on your e-reader. Don't put it off until later. Sing at the top of your voice in the shower and ignore the raised eyebrows of your family. If you like sport, find a release valve that gives you pleasure. Maybe the weekly fitness club is what you are looking for or perhaps you are happy just swimming lengths in the local pool on Tuesday and Thursday evenings.

If you dream of finding a healthy balance in your life, plan moments of relaxation into your routine. If you don't do it, nobody else will do it for you. 'No time' is the most frequent excuse, but that is really no excuse at all. We all get 24 hours a day – and that's the same for everyone in the world. If other people achieve a good life balance in 24 hours, why can't you? Scrap your non-productive activities, ditch unhealthy eating. Take plenty of exercise and ask for help if you need it. Do you really have to do everything yourself? Perhaps your colleagues or your family can lend a helping hand. Say 'no' to some of the tasks people try to push on to you and change the habits that are holding you back. You will find a new freedom and a healthier, more balanced way to live your life.

NOBODY ELSE CAN BREATHE FOR YOU

Let's take another quick look in the coaching room, where Alice came to some interesting insights.

'It was the same thing again on Saturday evening, but this time I decided to sort it out for myself!' says Alice with pride, sticking her thumb in the air.

'I still had an awful lot to do before I went out to dinner with my friend, to celebrate our two years together. I went through my "to-do" list in my head: the dog still needed to be let out; I still had three mails to send; I mustn't forget to confirm an important appointment for next week; and I had promised to phone my sister, who is down in the dumps because her partner has just left her. Oh yes, I had also promised to send Agnes that cake recipe she needs for her party… So much to do and so little time…

And then I thought to myself: "What is the most important thing right now?" The answer soon followed. "That a relaxed Alice can enjoy a well-deserved meal with her boyfriend." So I ran upstairs and filled the bath. My sister and Agnes could wait until tomorrow. And the other mails were better done from work. While I sank into the delicious lavender bath foam, my friend stuck his head around the door. "Darling, I'm really looking forward to tonight." "Me too, darling," I answered with a smile. "Me too."

Hopefully, you have already discovered that you are often better able to be there for other people if you first take care of yourself. If you are not yet convinced, imagine yourself sitting at the front of an airplane.

Suddenly, there is an announcement that an emergency landing needs to be made. Fear is everywhere. You can feel it all around you. The first thing you want to do is help your family, but what did the stewardess just say? 'Please put on your own oxygen mask before you try to help others.' Which makes perfect sense, of course. You can't help others if you don't have any oxygen yourself.

You can't help others if you don't have any oxygen yourself.

 Coach yourself!

What empties your batteries?
How do you block out tiresome thoughts, so that you can enjoy yourself?
What does 'enjoying yourself' mean for you?
How often do you place the oxygen mask over your own mouth before you try to help others?
When is your next appointment with yourself in your diary?
What are two or three appointments with yourself that you could make right now?
Write down the insights that you will later include in your identity card.

SMILE AT YOUR REFLECTION IN THE MIRROR
The effect of a positive self-image

Note to the director
Caring for yourself means smiling at your reflection in the mirror each morning.

Every day when we get up we choose what to wear. We want to make a good impression. We make sure that the colours don't clash and that our outfit is suitable for the right occasion. While we are cleaning our teeth, we run through the day's calendar in our head. A hundred and one different thoughts flash through our mind, as we work our way through our morning routine. But one thing we usually fail to do is to stop and think about the mood we want to be in when we step outside.

What mood would you choose if you want to have a successful day?

Jules starts moaning, which has become a usual ritual at the start of each session. Nobody understands him, the world is a rotten place, no one in his office can be trusted, and even his wife is not being honest with him. When I question him further about these interpretations, he quickly runs into a brick wall. I ask him for specifics: names, dates, times, places... 'Who said that?' 'When was that?' 'How do you know that?' Jules gets stuck and cannot answer...
In my office I have a large moveable mirror. This strikes me as being the right moment to get it. Jules looks puzzled by what I am doing, but I carry on anyway. Once the mirror is where I want it, I ask him to go and stand in front of it. He has absolutely no idea what all this has got to do with coaching. But he soon will.
'What do you see in the mirror, Jules?'
'Myself, of course,' he answers, slightly annoyed.
'No, what do you really see? Look at the details. Your expression, your posture, your hands, the position of your head...'

'The corners of my mouth are turned down... my head also hangs down... I can see the frown wrinkles... '
He falls silent. 'What else?'
Jules struggles to take a breath, trying not to let his emotions get the better of him. He carries on with his description: 'My hands hang limply at my side... Hmm... I'm not enjoying this. What a bloody awful exercise!'
Jules looks at me angrily. He wants to return to his seat, but I ask him to stay where he is. I haven't finished yet.
'Jules, I'm going to ask you to change a number of things about your body position. Are you willing to do that?'
He nods.
'Straighten your shoulders, pivot your pelvis, lift your head to 90 degrees, relax your jaw muscles, curl the corners of your lips upwards...' Jules follows my instructions, and with each step I can see his eyes shine with more and more energy.
I ask him to repeat his moaning of earlier, to repeat it exactly, word for word. He immediately admits that this is difficult, if not impossible.
His body position has had an impact on his thoughts.

Are you aware of the impact that your body position can have on others, and on yourself?

 Do you sometimes give presentations at work? If so, use one of your existing presentations and give it as though you were standing in front of your colleagues. If you don't have a presentation, imagine that you are standing in front of a panel and are asked to introduce yourself.

Ask someone that you trust to film you with your smartphone while you are giving your presentation or introducing yourself. Afterwards, view the film without sound.

Do you see someone full of confidence who clearly knows what he is talking about? Someone who is open towards his public, who looks them in the eye? Where are your hands? How do you move?

Do the exercise again and watch out for all these things. Once again, view the film with the sound off. There is a good chance that you will see a very different presentation and a very different person. And there is an equally good chance that next time you need to give a presentation for real you will make a bigger impact on them.

The way in which you look at yourself has a similarly powerful impact. Who do you see when you stand in front of the mirror each morning? Perhaps you welcome yourself with a negative comment:
'Oh no, I look terrible!'
'Pfff... another day with difficult clients.'
'I wish it was the weekend, so nobody would bother me.'
'My boss will definitely have some negative comments on my work, he doesn't like me anyway.'

The way you greet yourself in the mirror has a big influence on the way your day will go. Are you happy with what you see or does your self-reflection get your day off to a bad start? From now on, think about this consciously each morning. When you get up and look in the mirror, give yourself a friendly 'hello sunshine!' Look at yourself carefully and say something positive:
'I'm glad to be spending the day with you again!'
'Gosh, I really slept well last night!!'
'Thank goodness that dream was just a dream!'
'I wonder what adventures I'll have today!'

Okay, we realize that having this kind of conversation with yourself can seem a bit strange at first.

But test it for a month: you will soon see that your life becomes much more colourful.

YOU CAN'T GAIN 10 KILOS IN 24 HOURS

So let's give it a try. Do you know this feeling?

You are standing in front of the mirror after a successful day. Your new project has given you wings. Your boss has made it clear that you are the right person for the job and your colleagues agree. You feel full of energy!

You look in the mirror and your eyes shine with pride. And when you look more closely, you see that you don't really look all that bad for your age. Those few wrinkles actually rather suit you and your figure hasn't lost its shape. You simply flash a smile into the mirror and say goodbye to your familiar reflection.

Nobody else can think or feel for you. Your own thoughts create your reality. If you decide to think negatively, nobody can stop you. You create your own world the way you want to see it.

The next day doesn't go quite so well. Your boss has clearly got out of bed on the wrong side this morning and your colleagues are all absorbed in their own work. Nobody seems to be interested in you. To cap it all, when you get home your neighbour phones with a whole list of complaints. You can feel your energy draining. Before you know it, you'll start feeling low on energy, somehow older. Standing in front of the mirror, you'll see a face that's worn down, with the corners of the mouth sagging downwards. What happened to yesterday's powerful, virile version of yourself? And where did all that fat come from? Oh no! You really need to go on a diet. The buttons on your shirt are almost bursting. You feel ugly and old.

Sounds familiar?
Of course, you know it's not possible: you can't age 10 years or put on 10 kilos in 24 hours.
It is all connected with our thoughts and what we say to ourselves.

So it's high time to be a little more friendly for ourselves.

Nobody else can think for you or feel for you. Your own thoughts create your reality. If you decide to think negatively, nobody can stop you. You create your own world the way you want to see it.

THE SUNFLOWER

 Jessie enters the room, cheerful as always. She sits down and I give her a cup of coffee.
While she takes a first sip, I give her a quick look. This is a woman who I really admire, for her laugh, her charisma and her positive approach to everything.
'How are you, Jessie?'
'Fine. I've had a few setbacks recently, but it could have been worse.'
'Like?'
'My dad's back in hospital, so I have to cross town once every two days to visit him. The traffic's a nuisance and it takes me a good two hours to get there and back. But at least it gives me a bit of time to myself in the car. Good music, thinking about fun things.' A smile crosses her lips.
'And work hasn't exactly been a walk in the park, lately. Since the new CEO took over, he has brought in all his old friends from outside. Things aren't looking too good for me and I wouldn't be surprised if I get laid off fairly soon.'
'Gosh,' I say, surprised at the calm way in which she can talk about these things.
'I keep asking myself: what's the worst that could happen? Not very much, really. It could even be a new start. Who knows what doors might open up for me?'
Jessie carries on like this for another ten minutes or so, always managing to see the bright side of every situation, like a sunflower that always turns its face towards the sun...

Have you ever noticed how an entire field of sunflowers turns to the sun? So why can't you convince yourself to do the same? Even on cloudy days, sunflowers turn towards the light and warmth. How do they do that? And what can you learn from them? It might seem impossible for you not to say something good about each and every day of your life. It might not spring to mind immediately. But if you think hard enough, you will certainly find something. Every day.

Even on cloudy days, sunflowers turn towards the light and warmth. How do they do that? And what can you learn from them?

The trick is to make a habit of it.

Imagine that before you go to bed each night you stand in front of the mirror and congratulate yourself for all the good things you have done that day. These things will then be stored in your unconscious, so that you can 'process' them further while you sleep.

The next morning, you will wake up with the same positive self-image in your head, which will give you extra energy and inspiration throughout the day. You can be certain that all the details locked away in your unconscious will find their way to the surface, as and when you need them.

In other words, it is very important to know that you can influence the thoughts inside your head. Our mind responds to everything we put into it, whether true or not.

You often hear people say: 'I am so (slow, stupid, lazy, etc.)', as though there is nothing they can do to change it. But nothing could be further from the truth. We have the ability to change 50% of the contents of the amygdala (the emotional centre in our brain). This means that we can control our thoughts and feelings, providing we train ourselves in the necessary techniques.

So make it a habit to load positive thoughts into your brain and remember to always use the present tense. In that way, your mind will assume that the things to which the thoughts refer are already taking place and will move into change-mode more quickly.

Look at your life and make a list of all the positive things you have done. Perhaps you have helped someone today. Or maybe you closed a big deal. Possibly you made a little time for yourself or even just played with the kids in the garden. Search for all the little things and give yourself a pat on the back. You deserve it.

> **Coach yourself!**
>
> What thoughts do you dress yourself with each morning?
> What are you good at?
> How do you greet yourself each morning in the mirror?
> In what ways can you influence your thoughts?
> Do you sometimes give yourself a pat on the back? How exactly?
> Write down the insights that you will later include in your identity card.

FIND YOUR STOP BUTTON
Sometimes you need to step out of the rat race

 Note to the director
Taking good care of yourself means that you sometimes need to put your troubles aside, so that your mind has the space it needs and can live in the here and now.

Just imagine. You want to stop your car but there is no brake. Or you want to empty your washing machine but the drum continues to turn. You want to put the vacuum cleaner away but it keeps on sweeping until the next time you need it!

Happily, all these machines have a stop button. But wouldn't it be nice if it was that simple with human beings? When you know you need a little rest, all you really want to do is settle down in a comfy armchair and forget about everything. But those same nagging thoughts keep buzzing around in your head. It almost seems impossible not to keep on thinking. And the harder you try, the worse it gets. Even so, it is important from time to time to give your mind a little breathing space, if you really want to be the director in the film of your life.

But it isn't easy. Are you also the kind of person who always wants to do everything at the same time? Eating in front of the TV. Making a phone call in the car. Cooking the evening meal while the kids are trying to tell you about their day at school. Sometimes there is nothing wrong with that. There are only 24 hours in a day and there are moments when we feel obliged to do certain tasks simultaneously. But can you really taste the delicate flavours in your food while you are watching an exciting series on television? And don't the kids (and other road users) deserve a little more attention than that? Of course, this is all part of life. We live from objective to objective, but instead of enjoying ourselves for a while once we have reached a particular objective, the compulsion to move on to the next one always seems to gain the upper hand. STOP!

We live from objective to objective, but instead of enjoying ourselves for a while once we have reached a particular objective, the compulsion to move on to the next one always seems to gain the upper hand.

From time to time, we need to jump off the carrousel of life. And to do that, we need to hit the 'stop button'.

BACK FROM THE OLD DAYS

Our thoughts often wander to the things that are occupying our mind. We make our 'to-do' lists or we worry about what people have said to us. Why did he say that? Did he mean this? Or did he mean something else? And what about that presentation you gave this afternoon: was it as good as it should have been? Perhaps the one you have to give tomorrow won't be much good either...

Imagine the following situation:

 You are sitting in the sofa with your partner. There is a glass of wine on the table and a romantic film on TV... Suddenly, a friend calls. He tells you he is in trouble. His wife has left him, and he stays behind with the three kids. He is at his wit's end and doesn't know what to do. For the next 30 minutes he pours out his heart to you. You listen sympathetically, give him some advice and try to cheer him up. After half an hour, the conversation comes to an end.

At this point, you can do one of two things.
Scenario 1: You go back to the living room but your head is still full of thoughts about your friend. You even carry on thinking about him later that night in bed. Of course, your romantic evening is ruined. Is that what you wanted? And did it help your friend?
Scenario 2: You go back to the living room and devote your full attention to your partner. You will think about your friend and a solution to his problem in the morning, when you have a fresh mind after a good night's sleep.

It is obvious that the second scenario is best. It is sometimes necessary to put all your cares and worries – and certainly the cares and worries of others – aside, so that you focus fully on living in the moment, in the here and now. You will feel better for it afterwards, and will be better able to help others as well.

Whenever your thoughts drift off, there is an easy way to bring them back to the present. It takes a little practice, but it is well worth the effort. So why not give it a try for a day or so? You will soon see that it works. The positive thing is that you will waste much less time worrying. Stressful thoughts keep on nagging at you, often without you being able to do much to solve them. And in the absence of a solution, your stress becomes even greater, so that in the end the problem in your head is bigger than the problem in reality.

> *Stressful thoughts keep on nagging at you, often without you being able to do much to solve them. And in the absence of a solution, your stress becomes even greater, so that in the end the problem in your head is bigger than the problem in reality.*

Imagine: in a week's time you have an important exam. You are feeling stressed. And because you know you always have stress before exams, this creates extra tension, which means that you feel even more stress.

If you make yourself consciously aware that the exam will ONLY take place next week and that your stress today can do nothing to change this situation, perhaps you will be able to relax a little, so that you can concentrate on the things that are important NOW: for example, more revision or perhaps eating a healthy meal and getting a good night's sleep, so that you can build up your strength for the big day.

By asking yourself what is happening at this moment and how you are experiencing it, you bring yourself back from the future to the present. In other words, you draw a boundary between then and now.

THE 'NOW' MOMENTS

When you are trying to achieve particular objectives, you often forget to enjoy the pleasant moments you meet along the way. Most of us have a tendency to check non-stop that everything is going the way we want. Have things lived up to our expectations or can we do even better? As a result, we are frequently confronted by annoying emotions, which impel us to immediately go in search of a new solution. For practical problems, this is often very easy. If we hear that our car is making a funny noise, we take it to the garage. If we have a leaky tap, we call the plumber. Unfortunately, it is less simple with emotions. The harder we try to solve them, the worse they become. Efforts to change things only make the situation more irritating.

The trick is to try and escape. When you look at the situation from a distance, you will probably think: 'What on earth am I making such a fuss about; this will soon pass!' or 'I'm just in a bad mood today and am probably taking things too seriously'.

By accepting the situation and its emotions, you lighten the feeling and get more breathing space, so that you can better analyze what is really happening. If you can let go of your thoughts for a moment and just enjoy the here and now, you will save yourself a huge amount of energy.

Does this all seem so difficult? Just take three minutes a few times each day to concentrate on your breathing. Look around you and focus on what you see. Or close your eyes and listen to the sounds of the moment. These are simple things that you can do everywhere: while waiting for someone, on a train, during the commercials on the TV, even on the toilet!

When you have done this consciously for a few weeks, you will notice that you can enjoy the pleasant moments that every day has to offer.

A relaxation technique that takes this a stage further is mindfulness. Mindfulness is not about taking a brief 'time-out' but is more concerned with conscious sitting or lying, and with observing our own thoughts without judgement. Thoughts that come and go. Thoughts that we can surrender, because we are consciously dealing with them.

Hundreds of books have been written about mindfulness. It is not our intention to discuss mindfulness techniques in detail here. We do, however, want to make you aware that there are simple ways to restore a natural balance to your life.

Above all, we want to let you know that in our hectic western society happiness is often to be found in the little things in life. How often have you driven home on automatic pilot? When was the last time you cleaned your teeth without thinking about something else at the same time? Do you cycle to the bakery without enjoying the wonders of nature around you on the way?

Even during the difficult moments in life, you can easily apply these techniques. If you hold the hand of a sick friend, just enjoy his presence and the warmth of the moment together. If you are listening to a boring lecture, occasionally look through the window to marvel at the wonderful colours of autumn. If your child is being difficult, don't get angry but just watch his behaviour, without judgement. If your partner is out for the evening, experience how it feels to be alone and to be able to do what you want.

If you hold the hand of a sick friend, just enjoy his presence and the warmth of the moment together.

We always worry about the things we don't have in life; sometimes we need to stop and be grateful for the things we do have…

Coach yourself!

When do you use your stop button?
Do you consciously live in each moment?
How do you do that?
How well can you feel your body?
How many stressful thoughts can you delete?
Can you describe what you are enjoying at this moment?
Write down the insights that you will later include in your identity card.

....

....

....

....

4. DON'T LET YOURSELF BE SIDETRACKED

You know who you are and what you stand for. You know that you need to take good care of yourself, so that you don't lose energy. It seems like you have everything you need to make something of your life. But be careful. Don't let yourself be sidetracked. We allow ourselves to be too easily distracted from our objectives by all kinds of different things: by what others expect from us, by prejudices, even by our own thoughts. We are (far too) happy to remain in our comfort zone and forget what we really want.

PUT YOURSELF BEHIND THE WHEEL
Live your own life and not someone else's

 Note to the director
You are the only person in control of your life. Make sure it stays that way. On this point, no compromise is possible! In this chapter, you can find out why.

If you want something, make sure it is something that YOU want and not something that someone else wants for you. If you play a particular sport, ask yourself whether this is because you really love it or because your mother pushed you into it. If you studied marketing at university, was this your choice or were you simply following your father's advice that 'this is best for you'?

Many of us have allowed ourselves to be sidetracked or misdirected in life by the words of others. Of course, other people's advice is not always bad. Perhaps it was a good thing that your father helped to set the course for you when you were a rebellious teenager. Maybe your mother's constant nagging to attend the weekly training helped to build your character. All these experiences have made you what you are up to this moment. But from this moment onwards, it is up to you to decide which course you want to set in your life.

If you play the piano because your sister talked you into it, you can now decide that you want to stop. Or you can decide to play a different instrument. Or a different type of music. One that you really like. Maybe jazz instead of the classical music you grew up with.

Are you still unhappy in that marketing job of yours? Then start exploring the other professional options that are open to you.

TIME TO SET YOUR OWN COURSE

Imagine that you suddenly find yourself in the middle of the Sahara. You look behind you and in front of you. You look to the left and to the right. All you can see is sand. Goodness knows how you got here or why, but here you are and you've got to do something about it. The only thing that can help you is the compass you just found in your pocket. And, fortunately, you somehow seem to know that the nearest town is somewhere to the south. So you focus on travelling in this direction, with the compass to help you. Suddenly, the desert wind begins to blow. You bend your body forward to face the wind, sand blowing ever harder into your face. But you keep your objective in mind and you don't deviate from your course.

This metaphor is designed to make clear to you that it is not always easy to stick to your chosen course. You will often encounter obstacles along the way and sometimes it is tempting to change direction. It demands a great deal of energy and effort to face up to these winds and sometimes your vision of where you want to go may become blurred. If the going gets too tough, why not take a rest for a while, or make a small detour that takes you out of the wind, but without losing sight of your chosen objective?

Let's return to our coaching practice, where David is experiencing difficulties of this kind. He graduated from university a few months ago, but found it difficult to get a job. He was finally offered a position in the accounting department of a major company, which is also the mother company of his parent's own business. Can you already hear some alarm bells ringing?

 'I'm glad that I've finally got work,' he says. 'It wasn't easy to find something.'
'And? What's it like?' I ask him. 'Okay,' he answers. 'Above all, I don't want to let my parents down. I can't afford to make a bad impression – for their sake.' I say nothing and jot down a few notes. After a brief pause, he adds hesitantly: 'But I feel so cut off from everything in that department. I need to have people around me...'

David has a double problem: 1. he doesn't want to make a poor impression in the company, because he fears this will reflect badly on his parents; 2. he doesn't feel comfortable in the department where he works. And we could easily add a third problem: it cost him a lot of effort to find a job, so that were he to lose this one he would be forced to go through that same difficult process again.

Faced with these problems, what should he do? Should he stay where he is? Should he just 'grin and bear it'? The answer is unequivocally: NO. He needs to find another solution, and preferably as quickly as possible.

How many people find themselves in the same situation as David, stuck in a job that doesn't really suit who they are? And how many stay in that job, often their whole lives, prevented by fear or false assumptions from finding something better?

What course does David want to steer and can he do that in the company where he currently works? If David was behind the wheel, then ideally he would be sitting in a car with more people. He needs others around him to function at his best, to exchange thoughts, to express his ideas out loud. That is his nature. He has an extravert personality. If he carries on working in the accounting department, where his colleagues focus on their own task in almost stony silence, he will soon find himself fading away, perhaps even sinking into depression.

As soon as David realizes this, everything will become easier. He will better understand the course he needs to set, the course that leads to the things that are important for him. In his case, he asked his managers for a transfer to another department. As a result, he flourished and was soon promoted. He is now doing very well – but this would never have happened if he simply stayed where he was and done nothing.

It takes a lot of energy to know which course you want to steer, but it is important to take the time and make the effort to do it. After all, you are leading your own life and it is you who sits behind the wheel. Your parents and others around you will always want what's best for you and often think they know what's best for you, but these are things you must decide for yourself. And once you have done this, be confident that you will reach the objectives you have set. This will sometimes mean that you need to make difficult decisions, but making no decision is far worse than making the wrong decision. At least, then, you will have tried and will be able to learn from your mistakes, so that next time you can take the right step forwards. And always remember this important tip: never make compromises when it comes to setting your own course.

It takes a lot of energy to know which course you want to steer, but it is important to take the time and make the effort to do it.

LEARNING FROM THE PAST TO DIRECT THE PRESENT

It is nine o'clock in the morning and I have my first coachee on the line, who I am guiding through a leadership trajectory. William works for a large international company in Geneva. This is our first conversation. Before we discuss the results of his profile, I tell him something about myself and ask him to do the same. William says: 'I was born in Taiwan. My mother was a cleaner in the small restaurant where my father worked as an assistant cook. Their dream was to leave Taiwan and come to Europe, and they worked day and night to make this possible. They wanted to give me a better life. When I was twelve, we got the chance to emigrate to Austria, thanks to a cousin of my father. Once we arrived, my parents both found jobs in a Chinese restaurant.

They worked hard to pay the expensive fees for my private school. I was well aware of the chance they had given me and I wanted to make a success of it. At school, my friends knew little about my life. I spoke to them in German and English, but at home I still spoke Mandarin. I had – and still have – two names. I often had the feeling that I was living a double life. This feeling was strengthened when I went to study in America for my MBA.

Now I'm working here in Geneva, but my parents are still in Austria. I am slowly beginning to realize that the course I want to set for myself is very different from what my parents want. But that's still where my roots are. I often ask myself how I can bring my two worlds closer together.'

William's parents gave him the chance to study and he seized that chance with both hands, even though it wasn't always easy to reconcile the two different worlds in which he found himself. But he persevered and now he is steering his own course. The introduction he gave about himself immediately set the agenda for our following coaching sessions: how could William best use his life experience to have more impact as a leader? In particular, this experience means that he is capable of leading a very diverse team. In other words, his life so far has been a source of inspiration for setting his own course for the future.

Coach yourself!

Do you set your own course?
How do you do that?
Do you keep on believing in yourself?
How do you know that?
How strong is your sense of self-worth?
Do you let the wind blow you off track or do you stay on course?
In concrete terms, how do you do that?
How much influence does your family system have on your objectives?
Write down the insights that you will later include in your identity card.

....

....

....

....

....

....

....

....

....

INSTALL AN ANTI-VIRUS PROGRAMME

Your conversations with yourself have a bigger impact than you think

Note to the director

We have already talked about the need to take 100% responsibility for your own life. If you keep pushing responsibility for the things that happen onto others, you will never move forward. You are the director of your life, so if things happen it is up to you to decide how you react. However, 100% responsibility does not mean that you need to be extra hard on yourself.

Often we are harder on ourselves than we are on others. Just check the way you talk to yourself. Do you always criticize what you do or say or do you occasionally give yourself a pat on the back?

The inner critic in you forgets to install an anti-virus programme. As a result, critical thoughts creep slowly but surely into your mind, so that your internal conversations become accusatory rather than complimentary.

The inner critic in you forgets to install an anti-virus programme.

It's time now to get back to the coaching practice, where Gaby is waiting nervously. She is the sales manager of a large shoe wholesaler and has just received a sealed envelope from the company's HR department with the 360 degree evaluations that her colleagues have made about her. The intent is that she will look at the results and then take them with her next week, when she has her evaluation review with her boss. But Gaby first wants to discuss the comments with her coach: me.

'Okay,' I say. 'Are you going to open the envelope?' We look at the results together. They are neatly illustrated by category on a graphic, with headings such as 'customer-friendliness', 'computer skills', etc. The scores that Gaby has given herself are also shown, so that they can easily be compared with the scores given by her colleagues.

> I see Gaby catch her breath as she looks at the graphic. In nearly every category she has given herself a higher score than others gave her. At the end of the report, there is a section with comments. Her boss praises her for her efforts and for her excellent cooperation with both staff and customers. Her colleagues praise her for her expertise and her willingness to share it. Even so, I can see that Gaby's eyes are still focused on the graphic. 'What's going through your mind?' I ask her. She answers: 'Why couldn't I have been a bit more modest? My boss is going to think I'm a big head. I hope he's not going to show those results to my customers. They'll think I see myself as some kind of superwoman. What a disaster.'

Gaby is focused entirely on the fact that she rated her own performance too high. Her inner critic has taken over from her inner coach. Her thought processes block so completely that she doesn't even read the complimentary comments made by her boss and her colleagues. Her boss has written nothing negative about her; on the contrary, he has praised her across the board. But Gaby can't see that. She is much too busy criticizing herself.

It is to deal with situations like these that you need to install an anti-virus programme. Here are some tips.

STOP YOUR INTERNAL BICKERING
Before your emotional side starts to react, take a deep breath and say: STOP! Give it a try. Imagine that someone asks if you have already made the report of yesterday's meeting. The inner critic immediately begins to see the worst: 'Why is she asking that? You see, she thinks I am too slow. I should have made that report straight away and now I haven't got time'. When this happens, you should just pause, inhale deeply and say: STOP. The next time you receive a comment you don't like, just let things take their course. Go with the flow. One good trick – and an old one, at that – is to count slowly to ten in your head.

It is only from the moment we say STOP that we are able to take the next step of ditching the inner critic and turning instead to the inner coach. In this way, we take a decision not to criticize ourselves but to start a friendly conversation with ourselves.

WHAT INSTEAD OF WHY

When you are installing your anti-virus programme, it is useful to replace why-questions with what-questions. If we react to something emotionally, we usually have a tendency to ask 'why?' Do you remember Gaby's instinctive reaction: 'Why couldn't I have been a bit more modest?' But why-questions seldom solve the situation, because they are nearly always accusatory. This generally leads to a 'Why? Because!'-dialogue. 'Why is he doing this to me?' ('Because he probably thinks I deserve it.') 'Why isn't she listening to me?' ('Because she's always busy with her own thoughts.') Why-questions often result in because-answers and this does little to move situations of this kind in a positive direction. If you want to make progress in life, it is much better to ask what-questions.

Gaby would then no longer ask 'Why couldn't I have been a bit more modest?', but would instead ask 'What can I learn from the fact that I gave myself higher scores than the others gave me? Perhaps it says something about my positive attitude.'

By using alternative what-questions, your internal conversation becomes completely different. 'Why is he doing this to me?' becomes 'What can I do from now on to protect myself, so that his behaviour doesn't affect me so much?'

On a normal day, some 60,000 thoughts flash through your mind. 95% of these thoughts are neither useful nor new. As a result, you are wasting your time if you carry on thinking about them.

'Why isn't she listening to me?' becomes 'What can I do to attract her attention, so that she gets to hear my important message?'

EMPTY YOUR HEAD

On a normal day some 60,000 thoughts flash through your mind. 95% of these thoughts are neither useful nor new. As a result, you are wasting your time if you carry on thinking about them. What's more, if the 95% contains a lot of negative thoughts, your head will almost always be full of this negativism, so that you end up constantly criticizing yourself.

Imagine that you have a small rubbish bin on your desk. Every time you have a negative thought, lift the lid and drop it into the imaginary bin. You can even put a real pot or container on your desk. Nobody needs to know what it's there for. It is high time to get rid of all those useless negative thoughts. Just imagine the extra space you will create on the internal hard disc in your head. Suddenly, there will be plenty of room for more refreshing and inspirational thoughts.

YOU ARE YOUR OWN BEST FRIEND

Lisa is sitting in front of me with a dull look in her eyes. 'What are you thinking?' I ask her. 'I don't know what I want to do with my life. I have so little energy after my burn-out. I'm better physically, but I still keep worrying about everything. Why do I have so few friends? Why does nobody come and see me or ask me out? I feel so lonely. I have done nothing with my life...'
'Stop,' I say. 'We're going to look together to see how you can start talking more friendly with yourself.'

Saying 'stop' to your negative thoughts is the first step. As soon as you notice that you are overloading yourself with critical comments, you need to say the magic word: STOP! And you can easily do this for yourself, without any need for help from an external coach.

Once you have said stop, check to see how many times you used why-questions in your inner dialogue. 'Why do I have so few friends?' can become 'What can I do to get more friends?' or 'Where can I go to meet more people who have the same interests as I have?' 'Why does nobody come and see me or ask me out?' can become 'Who can I invite?' 'What can we do together this evening?'

Keep using these tools, because you won't master the technique all in one go.

Lisa certainly needs a rubbish bin on her desk. If you are someone who worries all the time, you need one as well. It helps to visualize where you can dump all the rubbish in your life, all those negative thoughts that are no longer of any use to you.

We are often too critical, too hard on ourselves and this prevents us from moving forward in life. It is vitally important to talk to yourself in the right way. From now on, try to be aware of this and remember: you are your own best friend!

Coach yourself!

How do you talk to yourself?
How often do you check your anti-virus programme and how exactly do you do it?
When was the last time you were harder on yourself than necessary?
What is the best way to interrupt yourself before you react?
How often do you ask why-questions to yourself?
How can you reformulate these questions?
How do you empty your head?
Write down the insights that you will later include in your identity card.

....

....

....

....

DON'T CLIMB TOO QUICKLY UP THE LADDER
How prejudices can sabotage you

 Note to the director
Prejudices can be a creeping poison that forces us off course, away from our objective. We need to be constantly on our guard against this.

When people start to judge before they have taken the trouble to learn the facts, then we can speak of prejudice.

Some examples:
'Wow, he's in a bad mood; you can see it in his face.'
'How can she lead a team? She's only got a secondary school diploma!'
'That woman's always laughing. She must be a happy soul.'
'He'll never be able to do it; he's so clumsy.'
'My proposal will be rejected; it always is.'

Prejudices! We've all got them… Michael Hall (Executive Director of the International Meta-Coach System) expresses it as follows: 'We are Meaning-makers'. It is impossible for us to look at something without forming an opinion about it. We are programmed to judge. This is one of the characteristics that make us human. Judging is one thing, but we must make every effort not to condemn on the basis of those judgements: not ourselves and not others. The more we question our own thoughts and opinions, the more filters we will be able to remove and the broader our view of the world will be.

In this chapter, we want to look more closely at this subject. If we have prejudices, we respect neither our own dream nor the dreams of others. We either make them too rosy or too sombre, because we are too quick to 'judge'. It is almost as if we want to quickly hammer in a nail before we have assessed whether or not a nail is really necessary or appropriate.

> *If we have prejudices, we respect neither our own dream nor the dreams of others.*

If we know the drivers in our life, prejudices can either help or hinder us to turn them into concrete reality. In most cases, however, we are not even aware that we have these prejudices.

LIMITING OR HELPING BELIEFS?

Let's return to the coaching room for an example from daily life. Today's coachee is Chris, a European sales manager for an electronics company. He does his job extremely well and his turnover figures keep on increasing year after year. Even so, he still doesn't feel completely happy.

 'I've been doing the same work now for 15 years,' says Chris. 'I'd like to do something different.' He looks thoughtful. 'Purchasing, perhaps. But that will never happen.'
I look at him, dozens of different thoughts flitting through my mind, but I deliberately don't attach any judgement to them. Instead I ask: what makes you say it will never happen?
'I've worked in sales all my life and it's too late to change now. I'm good at it and it earns me a lot of money. I am not trained for a switch to the purchasing department. I would love to do it, it would be a new challenge, but I couldn't accept the financial consequences, because my salary would certainly be much less than it is now.'
While he is talking, I think back to our previous session, when he talked about the drivers in his life. 'Do you remember how last time we spoke about the adventurer in you and how you would like to see more of him?'
Our conversation suddenly moves in a new direction…

Discovering and dealing with limiting beliefs is a regular theme in coaching sessions. In this example, Chris has a number of these convictions. 'I've worked in sales all my life.' How should we interpret this sentence? If it is a limiting belief, then the thought says: 'I have worked all my life in sales and it's too late to change now.' If, however, you transform it into a helping belief, then it says: 'I've worked my whole life in sales and now I want to see more of the adventurer in me. It's time for a change'.

Limiting beliefs stop you from reaching your real drivers and your true identity. They are sometimes difficult to identify, so it takes a bit of practice. But once you become aware of them, you can transform them into beliefs that can help you to lead the life you really want to lead.

There are other limiting beliefs in Chris's example:

'If I would transfer to a job in purchasing, my salary would certainly be much less than it is now.'
'It will never happen, because I've absolutely no training for it.'

Once again, it is possible to look at these convictions and re-programme them in your head.

'It is possible that I will earn just as much in purchasing as in sales.'
'I know how customers think, and I could also use that knowledge effectively in the purchasing department.'

BE AWARE OF YOUR PREJUDICES

How can you become more aware of your prejudices? To do this as objectively as possible, it is best to try and stick as close as you can to the facts. But that sounds easier than it really is.

Chris Argyris, a former professor at Harvard University, conducted a lot of research into the ways people learn and how prejudices first arise. One of the models he developed was the 'climb the ladder' model. According to Argyris, we sometimes climb up the ladder too fast.

» The first rung on the ladder consists of the facts. Each of us focuses on specific elements in any given situation, depending on our personal environment, our surroundings, and our norms and values. Take, for example, a set of traffic lights. We select the colour of the light as our focus. We need to be aware that we have 'learned' to look

at the colour of the lights. We could just as easily look at the stripes on the pole holding up the lights.
» The second rung on the ladder are the conclusions we draw from the facts we have selected. We know that a red light means 'stop'.
» The third rung on the ladder are our convictions. 'It is important to stop if the light is red, so that accidents can be avoided.'
» The fourth rung on the ladder are the prejudices that can result from our conviction. 'It is wrong to drive through a red light.'

In relation to ourselves and others, it is important to be aware of these four steps. If this is not the case, misunderstandings can easily arise.

On which rung of the ladder are you standing?
Do you stick with the facts or do you jump to conclusions, convictions or even prejudices?
If your partner asks 'Are you wearing a new dress?', do you stay on the first rung ('He is just asking if I am wearing a new dress, nothing more') or do you immediately jump to the third rung ('He thinks I'm spending too much money again!')?
If your wife asks whether you have already showered, you can answer simply 'yes', 'no' or 'not yet, dear' (first rung) or else you can glare at her angrily, while thinking 'What the hell have women got against men playing sport together? After all, she goes every week to that damned tennis club with her friends.' (fourth rung).

CULTURAL DIFFERENCES

Sometimes the situation is less clear. Cultural differences are a good example. Imagine that you are in Japan and give a gift to someone who has invited you for dinner. This person immediately puts the gift aside.

As a European in this situation, your thoughts probably match the following pattern:

Rung 1: selection of the fact: he takes the gift and puts it aside.
Rung 2: conclusion: he is not interested in what's inside.
Rung 3: conviction: he attaches no value to our friendship.
Rung 4: prejudice: Japanese people are impolite.

If, however, we know that it is normal practice in Japan to put any gift you receive aside, then our pattern of thought will be very different. We will just stay with the fact that our host has put the present aside, because we know that local custom demands that he opens it later and that this in no way indicates a lack of respect for our friendship. This shows just how important it is to stay with the facts, especially in new or strange situations.

Recently, there was an article in the newspaper about an airplane that returned to its home airport after one of the female passengers grew suspicious about the person sitting next to her during the flight. The man in question had dark, curly hair and a beard. He immediately started talking to his neighbour in a strange tongue, after which he began to scribble notes in illegible symbols on a pad. The woman found this strange, even disturbing, and so she confided her fears to one of the stewardesses. When she reported this to the captain, he decided to return to the airport from which they had just taken off...

Afterwards, it became apparent that the man was a famous Italian economist, who spoke English with a heavy Italian accent. The 'illegible symbols' were mathematical calculations that he wanted to note down before he forgot. Fortunately, he thought it was funny when they explained the situation to him.

Making people aware of their prejudices is a very important aspect of coaching. Do you want to look for the prejudices in the following example?

The people following the course are divided up into groups of two. Each participant must take it in turn to talk for ten minutes about an activity in his or her life. The other person must note down the prejudices that come to light during their partner's talk. It is not an easy exercise. Laura and Susan form one of the groups. Laura talks first.
'Tomorrow, I have to give a presentation. I have prepared a long introduction with lots of details, because they are all engineers.'

'That's the first prejudice,' says Susan with a laugh. 'Who says that engineers are interested in long introductions with lots of details?' 'You're right!' says Laura. She pauses, a thoughtful look on her face.

'But perhaps I don't know enough about the subject, if they press me closely on some points.'

'There you go again!' says Susan. 'Second prejudice: Why do you automatically think they are going to press you?'

'Well, they're bound to be critical – engineers always are, especially when they're all men.'

'Wow, two prejudices in the same sentence! First you assume that engineers are critical and then you assume that men are more critical than women?'

'Yes, that's what I assume. But of course, I can't know it for a fact...'

It is amazing how quickly people climb up the ladder of prejudice. So next time you catch yourself jumping to a hasty conclusion, take a step back and ask yourself: 'On the basis of which fact(s) have I made this judgement?' Before you start to judge, always make sure you have understood the relevant facts correctly. It will save you from a lot of potentially embarrassing situations and poor decisions.

The words 'Mama, why is that man wearing a jacket without any sleeves? Is he too poor to buy a whole coat?' are only amusing if spoken by a child.

'Got a new car? I suppose the other one was too expensive for you to keep on the road' is an implication that your friend will probably not be happy to hear. He may indeed be going through a bad patch financially, but he may just prefer his new car to the old one. You don't know, so don't make assumptions.

'It must be a great feeling, having a second child on the way' is something people only want to hear if a second baby is indeed expected.

Watch out for prejudices, but be aware that we are all guilty of them at some time or other. So remember not to judge people too harshly if they begin to show their prejudices towards you. Just suggest to them calmly that the situation is perhaps a little different from what they might think. Remember the four rungs on the ladder. You know that you sometimes climb this ladder too quickly, so it is only to be expected that your colleagues, partner, parents, friends, etc. will do the same. They often speak from ignorance and usually it is enough just to point out the real facts to them. Don't let yourself be caught out by the prejudices of others and certainly don't allow them discourage you.

Don't let yourself be caught out by the prejudices of others and certainly don't allow them to discourage you.

Above all, don't let prejudices – your own or other people's – determine the path you follow, because they can be a serious hindrance that may prevent you from listening to your real drivers, which is the only way to make your dreams come true.

 Coach yourself!

Which beliefs enable you to make your dreams come true?
Which beliefs do you no longer need? How can you transform these beliefs, so that they can still help you on your way?
How quickly do you climb the ladder of prejudice? Give an example.
Try and spot your prejudices in the days ahead. What do you see, hear and feel?
The next time you get worked up about something describe the different rungs on the ladder.
Write down the insights that you will later include in your identity card.

....

....

....

SEE THE WORLD REGULARLY UPSIDE DOWN
If necessary, look at things from a different angle

 Note to the director
'Just act normal; that's crazy enough already.' How often did our parents used to say this to us when we were kids? We played outside and thought it was great fun to bend over and see the world upside down.
How long ago is it since you last did anything like that? Surely you're not someone who just wants to stay nestled in his comfort zone? You still want to chase your dream? Don't get sidetracked: read this chapter.

Sometimes you feel that you are set in your ways. You ask yourself if this is all there is. But you forget that this is a situation you have created for yourself. You chose that field of study, you accepted this job, you proposed to your partner and together you decided to have children… You finally reach a point when you ask why your 'ideal scenario' of the past is no longer quite so ideal today. If you look back on how your life story has developed, you will always be able to find lots of happy events, but there will also be lots of other things that you now wish you had done differently. That's life. And you're not the only one who feels that way.

Doing things differently than others takes a lot of courage. It makes you more visible, more easily seen. It takes you out in the open and you can no longer hide the way you did before.

Borders represent clearly delineated ideas and clearly defined situations. We learn about borders when we are young and we know that they can play a useful role in our society. On the other hand, we also know that they can have a limiting, confining effect: they prevent us from seeing what might be possible beyond the borders.

Doing things differently than others takes a lot of courage. It makes you more visible, more easily seen. It takes you out in the open and you can no longer hide the way you did before. And this worries or intrigues many people.

Each time Greg enters the room, I think: What an impressive man… He is not only physically tall, but also has a voice and a smile that make a lasting impression. I'm certain I'm not the only one who feels this way. Without realizing it, he commands respect.

He is the head of an important department in a Belgian state ministry and I have known him for several years. He recently emailed me to ask if I would like to be his coach. When I asked him why he chose me, he answered: 'You're different. You dare to colour outside the lines. You have the guts to make me sweat…' That was enough for me. I took on the job and I did indeed let him colour outside the lines – both literally and figuratively. I gave him coloured pencils, asked him to draw, gave him exercises, went for walks with him, let him rediscover himself… But when the conversations went deeper, this highly rational man always laughed away his own feelings. 'I don't have time for feelings. Feelings are for other people.' One day, I gave him a task to complete at home. 'We will take it one step at a time,' I said, 'but you need to learn how to feel again.' I waved a large bottle of body lotion under his nose. 'From now on, you're going to use this body lotion every single day and I want you to concentrate on what you feel while you are rubbing it in.' He looked at me as though I had gone crazy, but he promised to do what I had asked. After that, our conversations got better and better. By carrying out the task I had set him in a disciplined way, I was able to bring him back via physical awareness to a new awareness of feeling. This made it easier in the following sessions to discuss his emotions in more detail. Step by step, as I had promised, he rediscovered his true self, thanks to my somewhat 'unusual' method. Unusual or not, it worked. This was an active coaching trajectory with a major impact.

Sometimes you need to do something 'crazy' to achieve the results you want. So don't be afraid to look at the world upside down every now and then…

DARE TO QUESTION

How much do you like living in your comfort zone? It is easy to let things tick over normally, because that's the way things are supposed to be. Your life continues without any comments from those around you. But one thing is certain: if you keep on doing the same old thing, you will keep on getting the same old results, time after time after time.

If you want to achieve a different result, you will need to do what you once did as a child: bend over and see the world upside down.

Because one thing is certain: if you keep on doing the same old thing, you will keep on getting the same old results, time after time after time.

Perhaps you only need to make minor changes. Perhaps you're ready for something completely new. Perhaps you want to go back to college, or redecorate your house from top to bottom, or broaden your circle of friends, or take up a new sport, etc.

Just because most people do something a certain way does not mean that you need to do it the same way. Everyone is unique, including you. So do things your own way! Test your boundaries and have the courage to break out of your comfort zone. Who knows what you might find.

COLOUR YOUR OWN WAY

If you are not used to colouring outside the lines and if you have no idea how those around you will react, there is obviously no need to turn the world upside down all in one go, unless you really want to. Maybe it's a good idea to start by just colouring outside the lines in your head. This will be your secret, but it will still work to inspire you.

Take your time. Try to look at things differently from others. The urge to carry on doing what we have always done is often an unconscious one. We fail to realize that it doesn't always have to be that way. So take a step back and ask yourself what would happen if the manner in which you currently do things was no longer an option. You will discover that your brain soon sees other options outside the lines. How would Donald Duck react in this situation, or Richard Branson, or your favourite pop star. You will be amazed – and amused – at the answers you get. Looking at things upside down really can be fun. Not to mention instructive.

It can also sometimes happen that circumstances force us to colour outside the lines. For example, if we unexpectedly lose our job. And, curiously enough, it usually works.

The urge to carry on doing what we have always done is often an unconscious one. We fail to realize that it doesn't always have to be that way.

Here are some more examples. You do an update on your computer and you notice that a number of the functions have changed. To begin with, this is troublesome, because things no longer work the way you want them to. But you don't have a choice: the options you once had within the lines are now closed to you. As a result, you need to search for new options outside the lines, and so you press on. Once you find these new options, they quickly become second nature. In fact, you are now able to do more – and do it better – than you were ever able to do in the past.

Or perhaps you have an appointment in town and you drive automatically to the destination, which you have already visited many times before. But today there are unexpected road works. Your sat-nav is useless and keeps sending you round in circles. Even so, we bet that you will still make it to your appointment on time. How? By looking at things differently...

Coach yourself!

When did you last view the world upside down?
Do you prefer colouring inside or outside the lines?
What small change in your life could make a big difference?
Look for examples of situations in which you were forced to see things differently.
How do you regularly adjust the ideal scenario of your life?
Write down the insights that you will later include in your identity card.

....

....

....

....

....

....

....

....

....

YOUR IDENTITY CARD*

You have now read 'I am'. The previous chapters have given you more insight into who you are and what is important for you. Before you start with 'I do', we would like to ask you to fill in the identity card below.

At the end of the 'I do' chapters, there will be another set of questions to see if you are ready to be awarded your director's diploma. But first it's time for your identity card, a necessary prerequisite to know who you are as a director. The answers are okay as you fill them in. In this questionnaire, there is no such thing as right or wrong. After all, every director is unique.

Who are you today?
What are your drivers? What makes your heart beat faster?
What makes you happy?

....

....

....

Do you listen enough to your heart? What is it saying today?

....

....

....

* For an electronic version, send an email to info@qlick.today

How do you treat your body? Diet, exercise, breathing, rest?

....

....

....

Are you the same person at home as you are at work? Which parts of yourself do you show to the outside world? Which parts do you keep private?

....

....

....

What are your strengths? Name at least five.

....

....

....

What do you experience as your weaker points? Name at least five.

....

....

....

Who are you when you 'do' nothing?

....

....

Who would you like to be in the future?

Imagine how you would like your life to be in five years' time and answer the following questions (if you want to make the exercise more challenging, think ten or even fifteen years ahead).

Think about your drivers. How can you best use these to secure the future you want? What is the difference between what you find important today and what you will find important in five years' time?

....

....

....

What will you need to carry on listening to your heart in the future?

....

....

....

What efforts are you prepared to make to get or keep your body in top condition?

....

....

....

How would you like to be seen in the future, both at home and at work? What do you want to show people?

....

....

....

What would make your life more valuable?

....

....

....

What prompted you to read this book?

....

....

....

What will you take with you from this first part, 'I am'?

....

....

....

Date   Signature

....

1. PRESS THE PLAY BUTTON

After reading part 1, you now have your own identity card. You have a better idea about your drivers, your values and your beliefs, about the things that are important for you. You know who you are and this allows you to set more concrete objectives in your life.

But now it's time to press the play button.

AND... ACTION!

 Note to the director
In this chapter, we will give you three golden tips to help you initiate action more effectively. Action that will allow you to 'do' as you 'are' – because this is the best way to reach your objectives.

You probably know the type. People with ambitious plans, who tell enthusiastic stories about the projects they want to implement, but whose words turn out to be little more than hot air. They usually begin their sentences with phrases like 'I will...', 'If I...' or 'I will try...'.

If you want to reach an objective, there is only one way to do it: by taking action. But often we wait far too long, so that the opportunity slips by. We wait until we have saved more money, until the children have grown up, until we have permission, until the right person or the right moment comes along. But we are afraid we are going to have to disappoint you: there is no such thing as the right moment.

When you want to reach an objective, there is only one way to do it: by taking action.

Successful people know when they need to press the play button. They don't like overthinking the situation. They develop a plan, check to see if it is feasible and then they act: without delay. When you take action, things happen. You set wheels in motion, you get the ball rolling.

When we want to start something, we often find ourselves blocked by a variety of different factors. But there are a number of simple principles that can help you to bypass these obstacles.

1. Don't be put off by the fact that the top of the mountain seems such a long way; plan to reach the summit – your final destination – step by step.
2. Reaching the summit alone is a lonely business. If you reach it together with others, you will feel more supported, make faster progress and enjoy the view much more intensely when you get there. But to reach the summit together, you first need to be able to enthuse others for your plans.
3. If you come across an obstacle on your climb to the top, don't be discouraged. Work your way around the obstacle. And if you don't succeed at first, try again.

STEP BY STEP

Do you know that feeling when you sometimes can't see the wood for the trees? You have planned everything perfectly and are convinced that everything will go well, but suddenly something happens that blurs the whole idea in your mind. You no longer have a clear overview of the project and it becomes increasingly difficult to see some structure in your work. Tension mounts and your fear of failure slowly stifles you... Sounds familiar? This is the moment when you need... vegetable soup!

Think about vegetable soup. When we eat it, we know that this soup is healthy and nourishing, but it is impossible to distinguish the flavours of the individual vegetables.

If you find yourself in a position where you feel you are losing sight of the big picture, remember our vegetable soup. Just because you can't taste the flavour of the individual vegetables doesn't mean they are no longer there. Just because you have lost the overview, it doesn't mean that it's gone.

When this happens, it is important to go back to basics and review things from the start. Which different vegetables did you put in the soup? Place them alongside each other on your work surface. Cut them up one by one. Give full attention to each of the different ingredients. It is only when you appreciate the worth of each element individually, that you will truly enjoy your vegetable soup.

 Note down your final objective as clearly and as concretely as possible, including all intermediary steps.

> An example:
> You want to improve the service in your company. That is a highly abstract objective, something that you can't simply 'teach' your team. 'Better service' is not tangible, so you need to make clear exactly what it means to you:
> » Staff is friendly and attentive.
> » The customer must never be kept waiting and must be given a clear and complete answer to his query.
> » Staff informs new customers that an after sales service is available.
>
> By splitting up your abstract objective in this way, you can set a series of smaller and more concrete objectives.

ENTHUSE OTHERS FOR YOUR PLANS

Enthusing others is not always easy. If you are more introverted, this will cost you a lot of energy. Even so, it is important that you are aware of the importance of involving others in your plans, preferably as early as possible. In our practice, we often see leaders and entrepreneurs who have worked out an entire action plan all by themselves. They know exactly what they want and how to get it. Unfortunately, their staff know none of these things; they have been kept completely in the dark. This can lead to problems when the moment comes to implement the plan.

Let's have another look in the coaching room, where Julie's case can illustrate exactly what we mean. Julie runs a successful catering company but has problems keeping staff. Several of them resigned last year, but she has no idea what she is doing wrong or how she can stop the leakage. And so she turned to us for help. It soon became clear why some people find it hard to work with someone like Julie...

Julie is a creative jill-of-all-trades. Happy-go-lucky, quick, assertive and full of bubbling ideas. Of course, there is nothing wrong with that – were it not for the fact that Julie always assumes that her staff will instantly understand, approve and perfectly implement all her brilliant plans, even though she takes little or no time to explain them. This often leads to confusion. Mistakes have been made and customers have been lost. As a result, tension increased in the team, to such an extent that some team members decided it was time to look elsewhere...

 Julie shows me a photo of her team with pride.
'This is my wonder team. They are fully behind my plans for the future. Who would have thought it after all the trouble we had last year? I have learned a lot since then,' she says, more to herself than to me.
'Now I always take the time to put my plans on paper, so that they are clearer and easier to understand. If I want to launch a new idea, I first look for images to illustrate what I mean. Only then do I draw up an action plan, which I discuss with my people. Once everyone has all the information they need, we organize a test. We lay the tables, serve the meals, take photos, just like we would for a real customer. Then we discuss the results together. And it works! We make fewer mistakes and all the team are 100% behind all my crazy ideas. It's great!'

Everything begins with a thought, an idea – your idea. Before you ever mention this idea to anyone, it has probably been bubbling away inside your head for weeks, if not months. Because you have been thinking about it almost non-stop, you have a very clear picture of what your idea involves, right down to the smallest detail.

That's good, but be careful. What seems crystal clear to you might seem as clear as mud to your colleagues. So don't expect them to immediately understand your intentions. Take the time to explain, so that they can see things the way you see them. This is the only way to get the results you want.

DON'T GIVE UP TOO QUICKLY

Once you have found the courage to go for your objective, you will inevitably find a number of obstacles along your way. These obstacles will slow you down and you may start doubting yourself. Have I made the right decision? Am I the right person to see this project through? Your head will be full of questions and these questions can quickly turn to fear, so that your self-confident 'I am' is turned into someone much less sure of him/herself. This is the point at which many people decide to give up.

But not you! Keep on believing in yourself and keep your focus fixed firmly on your objective. Ask yourself other, more positive questions, like those we learned in part 1. Instead of asking 'Why are things so difficult?' ask 'What have I failed to explain clearly?', 'What information are people lacking?', or 'What can I do to improve the situation?'

If you succeed in working your way through this difficult period, you will feel even more satisfied at the end of the road.

Coach yourself!

How can you transform your dream into a plan?
What are the different steps in your plan?
Is your plan clear and detailed enough? When do you involve others in your plan? How do you make them enthusiastic for your ideas?
What are the obstacles to your plan and how do you overcome them?
How can you make sure you carry on believing in yourself?
What tools can help you?
Write down the insights to take with you for your director's diploma.

2. 'DOING' FOR DUMMIES

If you know who you are, you will 'do' as you are. Your actions will reflect your true nature. Your 'I' is in harmony with your deeds. You get more energy and people can see it. You will feel happier and be more successful, both in your private and professional life. Because you know that you are pulling all the strings and have everything under control. You are the director – and you act like it.

The moment has now arrived for you to start working on it. And as we have already mentioned, this does not mean that we will be helping you to draw up your ultimate business or career plan.

No, what we are talking about is 'doing' for dummies, a 'back-to-basics' approach to your daily activities and your interaction with others. We are focusing on learning to listen (properly and authentically this time!), talking, asking questions and giving feedback. Because everything starts with good communication.

Once you have this, the rest will follow.

UNPLUG YOUR EARPHONES
Listening is more than waiting to respond

 Note to the director
When the Dalai Lama visited Belgium, one of his main messages was that people have forgotten how to listen. Most of us are preparing our answers while the other person is still talking. In our hectic modern world, we no longer know what listening really is. And even if we

unplug our earphones, we are still focused on our own music. Time for a change.

I am sitting in a team meeting and we are learning about our new CRM system. The trainer gives a summary of the different elements and explains the various processes. He shows us how we can log a new contact or draw up a tender. He goes through all the different functions, even including the bookkeeping. I can feel my energy draining.
I slept badly last night and I keep thinking about the dozens of emails I still need to answer today. My inbox is open, and while the trainer is explaining the different topics I take a quick look at my most important incoming emails and start to formulate one or two answers in my head. 'Are there any questions?' asks the trainer suddenly. His voice startles me and I realize that I have only heard half of his explanation.

There are different levels of listening and the lowest level is not listening at all. You have probably had meetings where your body is present but your mind is absent, so that you don't hear a word that is being said. Your thoughts are elsewhere. It is called *Mind travelling*.

Mind travelling is something that we are all guilty of from time to time. Your thoughts focus on something other than what you are supposed to be doing. It can happen while you are talking to someone, or while you are driving home from work, or even while you are watching the news on TV. If you make the effort to note down how often your thoughts wander in a day, you will be amazed at the result. We all know how wonderful it is to close our eyes and let our mind drift away while we are lying on a sunny beach on holiday. It is less wonderful when this happens in the middle of an important meeting where you really should be paying attention. If the boss suddenly asks you a surprise question while your thoughts are miles away, you could find yourself in a tricky situation!

There are different levels of listening and the lowest level is not listening at all.

The first requirement for listening properly is therefore the 'will' to listen, which in turn requires you to empty your head.

HOW DO YOU EMPTY YOUR HEAD?

Some tips for emptying your head:

» Sense how you feel. Are you in the right frame of mind to start a conversation? If not, adjust your thoughts. Make them more positive.
» Take all the time you need to land. When your conversation partner enters the room, create time, perhaps by offering him something to drink, so that you can both find the right level of energy before you start talking.
» When your thoughts wander during a conversation, write them down on a piece of paper so you won't forget them.
» Take a walk before you start an important conversation or meeting.
» Watch your breathing (remember the tips in the 'I am' section).

HEARING AND LISTENING

There is a big difference between 'hearing' – simply registering the message spoken to you by others – and truly 'listening'. If you listen properly, you not only hear the message but also understand it. It also means that you do much more than just listen to the words. Research by the Iranian-American psychologist Albert Mehrabian has shown that just 7% of our communication happens through words. Our intonation and other 'sound elements' (think of affirmative sounds such as 'mmm' or 'oh' or 'ah') are responsible for 38% of what we communicate, while the remaining 55% is communicated by our body language.

Real listening demands eye contact and positive body language. Have you ever noticed how you can tell from the posture of a person whether or not they are actually listening to you? For example, when you are talking, the chance is minimal that someone listens to you while he is reading an email or sending a message. Or pay attention to your own body language when you are talking. Your crossed arms may indicate to the other person that you are going to stick to your opinion, whereas a relaxed smile is more likely to show that you are open and curious about what he/she has to say.

If you want to have good contact with others, it is vital to show real interest and to listen. Remember that your conversation partner merits your full attention. In this way, it will become clear to your conversation partner that you are actively listening.

You can train active listening. It is one of the basic coaching skills.

 We are about halfway through the coaching session and Daniel is still talking nineteen to the dozen. He is explaining about his company and his plans to collaborate with an African partner. He outlines the problems he has already solved and how happy he feels with the outcome so far. I enjoy the way his passion shines through in everything he does. I make notes about one or two things in his story that have struck me as curious and ponder about how these things are linked to other comments he made in previous sessions. Occasionally, I ask a question. When he finally stops for a moment, I share with him what I have heard so far and also what I felt while he was talking. He looks at me, gives a confirmatory nod – and then carries on with his discourse. I continue to listen attentively and allow my facial expressions to show what I am feeling. After an hour and a half, as we approach the end of the session, I ask: 'Daniel, what can I do to help you further with all this?' He answers: 'Just carry on being what you already are: my soundboard. It's a relief to be able to talk freely, without someone judging what I say. I don't get a lot of opportunities to do that…'

DIFFERENT LEVELS OF LISTENING
Laura Withworth (an expert in co-active coaching) talks about different levels of listening.

Level 1: You only listen to the words and you hear what you want to hear, the things that are useful to you.

An example:
Speaker: 'I don't have the confidence to speak up in a meeting.'
Listener: 'Why not?'
Speaker: 'I get so nervous that I forget what I wanted to say.'
Listener: 'Oh, all you need is a bit more practice. I used to be the same, so I followed some assertiveness training, and it really helped.'

In level 1 you are listening, but your main focus of attention is on yourself. Your listening is more a matter of 'waiting for a chance to respond'. You think primarily about your own experiences and you are ready to give advice on this basis. If there isn't a lot of time and you need to give some advice quickly, this type of listening can be useful. But you need to realize that you have not been listening with your full attention.

Level 2: You focus on the other person and listen with all your senses. You put your own thoughts and opinions aside.

An example:
Speaker: 'I don't have the confidence to speak up in a meeting.'
Listener: 'Have you any idea why?'
Speaker: 'Not really. But I always get so nervous that I forget what I wanted to say.'
Listener: 'Are there some situations that make you more nervous than others?'
Speaker: 'Yes, if it's a large group. I find it much easier with smaller groups.'
Listener: 'And how do you feel in those different situations?'
(The listener keeps on asking questions.)

In level 2 you are focused completely on the other person and you listen with your full attention and all your senses. You don't give advice and your conversation partner sees that you are listening carefully. This level of listening is very useful, because the conversation partner feels that you are genuinely interested in him and what he has to say. As the listener, you ignore yourself completely: it is all about the other person.

Level 3: You focus on the other person and on yourself. It is only then that a true dialogue can take place.

An example:
Speaker: 'I don't have the confidence to speak up in a meeting.'
Listener: 'Have you any idea why?'
Speaker: 'Not really. But I always get so nervous that I forget what I wanted to say.'
Listener: 'Are there some situations that make you more nervous than others?'
Speaker: 'Yes, if it's a large group. I find it much easier with smaller groups.'
Listener: 'I see that you are balling your hands into a fist. Are you angry?'
Speaker: 'Of course I'm angry. I want to get rid of my fear!'
Listener: 'Yes, I can understand that. In the past, I used to be angry as well, when things didn't go the way I wanted.'
Speaker: 'Really? So you had the same fear? What did you do?'

In level 3 a real dialogue develops, because you are still listening with your full attention and all your senses (like in level 2), but now you are also saying what you think and how this makes you feel. In addition, you use your own intuition and check with the other person whether or not the things you have noticed are correct. As you can see from the example, this level of listening often sets the conversational ball rolling, with the speaker asking his own questions instead of just answering yours. This is what dialogue is all about.

From now on, ask yourself which level of listening is appropriate to the different situations in which you find yourself. In particular, practice level 2 if you want to learn how to listen better. You can also easily test how much improvement you are making. Each and every day, we all meet people who have something to tell us. But can you still remember what they said three or four hours later? Can you recall all the details? Start this exercise with your family and friends: active listening can make a huge difference in any relationship.

WE HAVE FORGOTTEN HOW TO LISTEN

Due to the speed of the world around us we have forgotten how to listen. We are much too focused on ourselves, so that we confuse listening with 'waiting for the chance to respond'. Most people ask no more than simply to be listened to. You have probably experienced this feeling yourself, and you can tell instantly when somebody is listening to you or not. So remember this when you are listening to others and make a real effort to understand what the other person wants to say. Focus your listening not only on the words, but also on the behaviour, movements and intonation. These latter aspects can also give you plenty of information. If your conversation partner has a twinkle in her eye while she talks about her hobby, you can be sure that she really enjoys it. If, however, she is constantly fidgeting or avoids eye contact, you may wonder what the reason behind this behaviour is.

Listening has almost become an art in our hectic world. How afraid of silence have we become? And what do we miss because of that?

Listening has almost become an art in our hectic world. How afraid of silence have we become? And what do we miss because of that?

So take a moment: stop what you are doing, put the book down... and listen.

Coach yourself!

How can I empty my head, so that I can better listen to others?
In what way does someone's body language demonstrate that he/she is truly listening to me?
How can I show someone that I am really listening to him/her?
Which listening level is easiest for me?
Which level(s) do I need to practice more?
In which situations do I want to listen better?
I make a list.
Write down the insights to take with you for your director's diploma.

....

....

....

....

....

....

....

....

....

PUT ENOUGH QUESTION MARKS IN YOUR SCRIPT
The power of asking the right questions

 Note to the director

In the next part of 'doing' for dummies we are looking at asking questions. Are you afraid to ask for a pay rise? Do you think it's 'not done' to ask your partner for help? Do you lack the courage to ask your friends' opinions about your new project? Take as your starting point this simple truth: there is no such thing as a stupid question. It is only by asking questions that you will ever get answers. And some answers can really help you along in life. Here you can read why and how.

EVEN IF YOU ARE AFRAID – ASK

How often do you have a question on the tip of your tongue but are too afraid to say it? Fear is often the biggest stumbling block to asking questions. You don't want to appear stupid, you are frightened of being rejected, you are perhaps even more frightened of getting a 'no' for an answer. It's a shame, because by keeping silent you let dozens of golden opportunities slip by.

A really powerful question can work wonders. You will be amazed by what it can set in motion.

By asking questions, you get information; information that is often very different from what you expected. Or as Philip Glass once put it: 'The question is the mother of the answer'. Think about why and in what way you ask questions. Make sure that your questions are real questions, without prejudice. A really powerful question can work wonders. You will be amazed by what it can set in motion.

There is nothing wrong with not knowing: you can just ask whether someone else knows the answer. Children are great at this, because they are not (yet) afraid of looking stupid. In fact, their ignorance prompts them to ask questions all the time:

'Mama, why are you peeling those potatoes?'
'So they'll be clean for us to eat, sweetie pie.'
'How come they're dirty, mama?'
'Because they come out of the ground.'
'So why do we eat them, if they come out of the ground and are dirty? You say I should never eat anything I pick up from the ground.'
'This is different, sweetheart. We can peel potatoes to make them clean and we eat them because they are nourishing.'
'What's nourishing, mama?'
…

This kind of conversation can go on for a while.

QUESTION WITHOUT PREJUDICE

'You'll probably be too busy to make an appointment, won't you?'
'I suppose I talk too much for an introvert like you?'

We often give our own answer in the questions we ask, so that we reveal our thoughts to our conversation partner. This type of question is not really a question. Real questions are neutral and show that you are prepared to receive any answer, even an answer you perhaps did not expect. If you find it difficult to put your own thoughts aside, it is better to first make a statement before you ask a question.
'I can see that you are running from one meeting to the next. Is it still convenient to make an appointment?'
'You are a lot quieter than I am. Does it bother you if I talk so much?'

THE RIGHT QUESTION FOR THE RIGHT ANSWER

What do you want to achieve with your question?
A short and sharp answer, a decision, information, the deeper reasons why a particular process went wrong, etc.?
There are different ways you can ask a question:

1. Closed questions

Closed questions are questions to which you can only answer 'yes' or 'no'. They are very useful if you want a quick answer or a decision.

'Is it all right for you if we discuss this tomorrow?'
'Are you home in time for dinner tonight?'

2. Open questions

When you ask questions with words like how, when, where, with what, in what way etc., your conversation partner cannot answer with a simple 'yes' or 'no'. These are open questions and they generally give you lots of information to think about. They are the questions that allow you to learn things – particularly when questioning people who are usually wary about the information they release.

Read the following case study carefully and note the different questions that are asked. What can you learn from this?

Peter is preparing for his annual evaluation review. He is a bit sceptical. How can his new boss, Ellen, know anything about his performance during the past year? She's only been in the job for a couple of months. To cap it all, she's also asked him to prepare a list of his objectives for the coming year. Peter feels uncertain about this. His ideas about what he wants to achieve next year are not very specific and he doesn't know how measurable he can make them.

When Peter enters Ellen's office, she is sitting comfortably in the corner, drinking a cup of coffee. 'What would you like to drink, Peter?' she asks. 'Coffee will be fine, thank you,' he answers. 'Please sit down, Peter. I'll fetch you one.'

Peter sits down in the chair next to Ellen's and spreads his papers out on the table in from of him. He's now feeling more at ease. Ellen comes back with his coffee. 'Milk? Sugar? I wasn't sure, so I brought both.' She sits down next to him. 'Since I've only been in this job for two months, it's difficult for me to evaluate your performance during the past year. So I've spoken to your previous boss and agreed with him that he will do your evaluation for the last 12 months. He'll be contacting you about that in the near future.'

Peter nods in approval. That sounds sensible. 'What I want to focus on in this conversation,' continues Ellen, 'is what you yourself can tell me about your performance over the last year. In which areas did you reach your objectives, where did you have difficulties…? That way, we might be able to jointly set you correct objectives for the year ahead. What do you think about this approach?'
Peter can feel the stress fading away and starts talking excitedly about a dozen different things at once.
'Is it okay if I write a few things down?' asks Ellen.
'No problem,' says Peter, and he carries on talking.
Ellen listens and asks questions:
'What do you see as realistic objectives for this year?'
'How do your objectives fit in with the company's overall objectives?'
'Have you thought about how you can make them measurable?'
'What can I do to help you reach your objectives next year?'
By the end of the conversation, they have agreed five realistic and measurable objectives for the coming year. Peter is more than satisfied and feels supported by his new boss.

By asking the right powerful questions, you will be able to come across as a credible and supportive leader. Far too often, we still consider questioning as a sign of weakness.

In the above example, questions were used for a number of different purposes: to reassure, to ask for information (and in that way to admit that you don't know everything), to ask for feedback, to agree the next step forward, to offer help...

Asking questions is a powerful tool for communicating with others. By asking questions, you receive valuable information, but it also has another beneficial effect. By asking questions, you give the

By asking questions, you give the other person the chance to find a solution. By asking questions, you create responsibility.

other person the chance to find a solution. By asking questions, you create responsibility.

'Ask questions' if you want to be the director of your own life and realize your dreams. 'Ask questions' if you want to enthuse others and involve them in your plans. 'Ask questions' if you want to inspire others to also become their own leader.

> **Coach yourself!**
>
> What stops you from asking more questions?
> How often do you use open questions?
> Closed questions? Write down a number of examples.
> When do you include your own thoughts in a question?
> How often have you asked a question today? What was the result?
> Write down the insights to take with you for your director's diploma.
>
> ....
>
> ....
>
> ....
>
> ....
>
> ....
>
> ....
>
> ....

FEED YOUR FELLOW (WO)MAN
Feedback serves to feed others

Note to the director
In this chapter, we are going to take 'doing' for dummies a step further. Because if you can master the techniques to listen properly and ask the right questions, you will also become a master in the giving and receiving of feedback. Successful people know just how powerful constructive feedback can be.

I have been given the task of strengthening the dynamics within a leadership team. In recent months, there have been a number of job changes. As a result, the team has a few new members, while some of the old members have moved on to new challenges in other departments. The training is taking place at an external location in the Belgian Ardennes. The participants from the company's different European operations all arrived last night, so this morning we can start bright and early. After a brief introduction, I get the ball rolling with an exercise: 'Imagine that we are all here at a cocktail party, where you will be meeting people you know.'
Some of the participants start grinning.
'In a minute, I am going to hand out a set of cards for each of you. Each card contains a description.' I read out one or two of the cards. 'Is always enthusiastic and can motivate others.' 'Has an eye for detail and always goes straight for the objective.'
I continue: 'Read each card and give it to the colleague you think best matches the description. If you are given a card, you have the option to accept it or not.'
To get things started, I take the first card and read it out loud: 'Always helps to create a good atmosphere in the team.' I walk across to the man who earlier came into the room singing and offered a cheerful 'good morning' to everyone present. 'I think this card fits you,' I tell him,

even though I have never met him before. 'Thank you!' he says with a big smile.

'FEED'-BACK SERVES TO FEED OTHERS

Feedback is often seen as criticism. In this chapter, we want to talk about the power of positive feedback and – in its superlative degree – the possibility of giving compliments. In some companies, feedback is still confused with the annual evaluation review, which is something most employees look forward to with trembling knees.

Fortunately, an increasing number of organizations are starting to focus on the personal development of their employees, giving them feedback all year round, almost on a daily basis, and not just at specific 'timetabled' moments.

In some companies, feedback is still confused with the annual evaluation review, which is something most employees look forward to with trembling knees.

The purpose of feedback is to nourish: literally, 'giving feed back'. It has a giver and a receiver.

As a feedback giver you may sometimes have the experience that you are not certain about the correctness of your input. Up to a point, this is not important, as long as you offer the feedback with the intention of helping the other person. In the above example with the cards, some people hesitated in the beginning to give cards to their colleagues, particularly since some of those colleagues were new. 'How can I know whether I am right or not?' some of the participants asked. 'Maybe he/she doesn't fit that description at all.'

We often hear this comment whenever we do the card exercise – until the moment when the players eventually dare to leave their comfort zone and get into the swing of things. When that happens, the atmosphere quickly improves and cards are exchanged faster than in a Monte Carlo casino. People are generally very grateful to receive genuine and constructive feedback.

As the receiver of feedback, it is obviously important that you are open to what the other person wants to tell you. Sometimes it can be a bit scary, if you know you are going to get some feedback, but you don't know what. This is a good moment to think about the example of the cards. You are not obliged to accept the feedback, and certainly not if you don't think it is useful or accurate. After all, you wouldn't swallow food that you don't like, would you?

NEVER SAY 'NO' TO A COMPLIMENT

If you get positive feedback, don't just brush it aside, as if it is nothing. If someone says: 'Well done, what a brilliant piece of work', don't answer: 'Oh, it was nothing. Really, I just happened to have the right information at hand.' Why not try and be more positive about it? You might reply (preferably with a big smile): 'Thanks a lot! I have a good feeling about it as well and I am glad that so many customers are satisfied.' In this way, you accept the compliment with both hands and also indicate to others your own level of self-worth. If you don't value yourself, how can you expect others to do so?

If you don't value yourself, how can you expect others to do so?

Even so, we still frequently reject the compliments we are given, largely because we don't know how to deal with them. And so we change the subject, start to blush, avoid eye contact, etc. We just don't know how to behave at such moments.

Imagine that someone gives you a present. You wouldn't immediately give it back, would you? Well, it's the same with compliments.

GIVE FEEDBACK ABOUT WHAT PEOPLE DO, NOT ABOUT WHO PEOPLE ARE

Whether you are a giver or a receiver of feedback, it is important to remember that you must always give feedback about someone's behaviour, and not about someone's identity. Givers still too often make comments like 'You are always late', 'You are always so stupid', 'You really are lazy', etc. Such feedback can seriously confuse the receiver. Instead of 'nourishing' us in the way we hoped, we accept the comments as criticism of our whole being. This can sometimes block our whole system or even make us ill.

If someone tells you 'I saw that you were late for the meeting this morning', how do you react? Do you regard it as a one-off occurrence ('Okay, so I was late for the meeting, but I was stuck in traffic because of an accident') or do you exaggerate it into something you carry with you for the rest of your days ('Yes, I was late for the meeting. I'm always late. I will never succeed in structuring my life...')

In this latter instance, you end up turning the same thoughts over and over in your mind, whereas this was probably never the intention of the person who made the comment.

 Some tips to give feedback in the right way.
Step 1: Start with the facts. Be as specific as possible: what, where, when.
Step 2: Name what you think or feel (this step has the most impact, because it shows how the situation affects you – so don't forget it!).
Step 3: Now give your nourishing feedback.

Example 1: (1) Last week you were 15 minutes late for the presentation in Brussels. (2) I thought it was a pity that you missed the introduction. (3) Perhaps next time you should take a different route to the conference hall.
Example 2: (1) When you entered the team meeting yesterday, you had a big smile on your face. (2) It immediately made me feel happy. (3) I think that you have a really positive effect on the atmosphere in our group when you start a meeting like that.
Example 3: (1) Mrs. Jones was in the shop yesterday to collect her package and I saw that you failed to open the door for her when she left. (2) That worries me, because we have already talked about the importance of a customer-friendly approach. (3) I'd like you to bear that in mind for the future.

From now on, try to deal with feedback in this manner. If, as a giver, your intention is genuinely to feed others – and this intention is crucial – nothing much can go wrong.

YOUR BLIND SPOT

John is one of my clients. As part of his coaching trajectory, we have agreed that I will observe him during a day's work at his office. On the day in question, he calls his staff together for a meeting in the conference room. He introduces me as his coach and says I will sit at the back of the room to watch how things develop.
During this meeting, John wants to get some ideas from his people about how they can increase their sales figures. The atmosphere is informal; even so, the discussions are intense. With one hand in his pocket and a pen in the other, John tries to write down all the ideas as accurately as he can on a flip chart. But whenever he writes something, I can hear the jangling of the loose change in his pocket. With every new thought he writes down, his right hand scribbles something across the page, while his left hand slips into his trouser pocket and plays with the coins it finds there. I can see how his staff look at each other and smile every time this happens; some of them even whisper to each other in amusement. When John has filled two pages with ideas, he sits around a table with his team to discuss them. Based on the best of the ideas, together they draw up an action plan to improve the sales figures. John asks if everyone is happy with the outcome of the discussion and his team all confirm that they are. John then asks me if I have any feedback on what I have seen. I tell him that I have no comments on the content, but would like to say something about his presentation style. I look at the group and say: 'I'm sure you all noticed what I noticed, so which of you can give John some useful feedback?'

Isabelle raises her hand to speak. 'John, do you know that you always play with the coins in your pocket whenever you write something on the flip chart?'
John looks amazed and pulls a handful of coins out of his pocket. Suddenly, everyone starts to laugh. John says: 'Thanks for the feedback. I had no idea I was doing that. I suggest that after work we use these coins to go and have a good beer!'
'And will someone please let me know if I ever do it again in the future. Goodness knows how many presentations I've already given to the board of directors with the sound of coins jingling in their ears!'

Feedback often has most effect if it relates to things that people are not aware of. Have you ever heard of a 'blind spot'? Blind spots are actions that you do not know you are doing – whereas they are blatantly obvious to everyone else.

Have you ever heard of a 'blind spot'? Blind spots are actions that you do not know you are doing – whereas they are blatantly obvious to everyone else.

You probably know someone who always uses the same mannerism when performing a particular action. Do they know they are doing it, or is this a blind spot? Perhaps you also have a blind spot? Biting your nails, jiggling your crossed legs, nervously creasing your forehead, running your hand over your hair, wearing a silly grin whenever you help someone... Wouldn't it be useful if people made you aware of these things?

In fact, you can never become aware of your blind spots unless people actually make the effort to point them out to you, and that's why they are called 'blind'. Or unless you ask them to do this for you. So give it a try. And do the same for them: help your colleagues to discover their own blind spots. They will be truly grateful.

If you are open for feedback, you will continue to grow as a person and perform better at your job. If the feedback is critical, try not to see it as a personal attack but as well-intentioned comments from which you can learn. If the feedback is positive, allow yourself to enjoy a brief moment of self-congratulation. After all, you deserve it.

> **Coach yourself!**
>
> How often do you give feedback?
> Do you know how you can give good feedback?
> How do you deal with feedback? Give an example.
> What are the blind spots of the people around you?
> How do you ask others to point out your own blind spots?
> What can you learn from this?
> Write down the insights to take with you for your director's diploma.

3. YOU ARE THE BOSS

In the previous section 'doing for dummies', we looked at a number of simple communication techniques that will make your interaction with others that much easier and more comfortable.

Say what you've got to say. And do good. We are now going to use the same techniques to really take the direction of your life into your own hands. Because you are the boss. You are the leader in your life. If that is your ambition, you must learn how to define your own boundaries; you must be able to determine what you want and to make clear to others what your wishes are. This is not always easy. Sometimes we are too modest or we don't dare to say what we really want. But in the long run this is not good, not for yourself, and not for others.

For that reason: say what you've got to say. And do good.

LEARN TO SAY 'NO'
How a 'no' can be a 'yes' for you

 Note to the director
We live in a world where everything happens at lightning speed. Professor Herman Van den Broeck of the Vlerick Leuven Ghent Management School has said that today people receive more information to process in a single day than someone living in the Middle Ages received in their entire life. What's more, we also have to fulfill a number of different roles: at home, at work, in our social life. As a result, it is important to learn how to say 'no',

when necessary: to relax, to find peace, to keep control.
If you fail to do this, you are not living your own life.

Do you sometimes have the feeling that the day just flew by? Does it seem like you have never finished what you have to do? Do you sometimes feel like a prisoner in your own life? There are deadlines to meet at work. Traffic jams stress you out on the way home. When you get there, the kids are demanding your attention all the time. To top it all, your social agenda is full to overflowing. You are often so busy that you lose sight of your own wellbeing. And even though you are unique, lots of other people face by this same problem. That's why there are so many burn-outs today.

Let's return once more to the coaching room, where Mary has a problem. She has lost control. See if you can think of possible solutions for her: what can she do to set her own boundaries?

'Now I've really had enough,' sighs Mary.
I can see from the expression on her face that she is tired. She has bags under her eyes and looks exhausted. Her shoulders are slumped down and she is leaning slightly forwards.
'My boss thinks that I can do everything. I've hardly finished one file and he's already waving another one under my nose. In the meantime, I have to answer the phone as well, not to mention being coffee lady for him and all his visitors.'
I want to ask her a question, but she hasn't finished yet.
'And do you know what's worse?' She looks at me as though I should already know the answer.
'As soon as I get home, my two kids are there, jumping up and down for me to play with them. Or else they want help with their homework. Or they want to tell me about their own day. To be honest, all I want is fifteen minutes of peace and quiet, a little "me-time" to recover from the stresses and strains of the day. Do you understand?'
I nod.

'Because I'm so tired, I can't immediately give my children the attention they deserve, which makes them even more difficult. Which in turn makes me feel guilty for not being a good mother... No, things can't carry on like this.'

For many people this is a recognizable situation. Pressure at work followed by pressure at home, where the kids want to tell their story and 'do things'. Exactly at the moment when you don't feel like it. Because all you feel is exhausted.

Take a few seconds to think what Mary could do to get her situation back under control. And then read on to learn what solution Mary found for herself.

I look at her and say nothing.
She continues: 'Perhaps I should give the kids something to do as soon as I get home. Draw a picture for mummy, something like that... They'd like that and it would give me a bit of time to come up for air. Maybe I could also stop work fifteen minutes earlier. There's no reason why I should always be the last one to leave. Then I could go for a short walk; that would help me to relax a bit and clear my head. And I really need to tell my boss that I can't do my own work and answer the telephone and do the coffee.'
Mary is lost in her own thoughts. Without me needing to ask a single question, she has found her own answers. Hopefully, she will now find the strength to turn those good intentions into reality.

A SMALL WORD THAT MAKES A BIG DIFFERENCE

Learn to say 'no'. No, you don't need to go to that business dinner. No, you don't need to take over that extra work from your sick colleague. No matter how difficult it can sometimes be, most successful people all know how to say 'no'.

If this is something you have trouble with, it is not easy to change things overnight. We realize that it takes iron-strong discipline. But if you can turn it into a habit, your life will become so much easier.

No matter how difficult it can sometimes be, most successful people all know how to say 'no'.

Some simple tips:
- Do you need some silence after a busy day? If so, allow yourself the luxury of a few moments for yourself. Go for a walk outside during your lunch break. Or agree with your partner that you need ten minutes of 'me-time' when you get home, after which your family will once again have your undivided attention. Your partner may need to get used to the idea, but he/she will soon see the benefits it has for all of you.
- Does everyone take it for granted that you are always instantly available? If so, put your telephone on hold for half an hour. Can 30 minutes without the phone really make that much difference? Not to others, but it can be a big help for you. One habit we use is to switch off our cell phones during mealtimes. Any important message can be left on voice mail, allowing us to enjoy a pleasant meal with our families.
- Make a deal with yourself; after all, you are important.
Don't forget that you are the director of your own film. If you want to do sport for an hour each week, note it down in your diary. If another appointment later needs to be made at that same time, you can then decide which of the two is most important. But let's be honest: what is more important than taking care of yourself?
- You can also make a short list of things that you want to stick to. This will help identify your priorities and give you clear guidelines for when to say 'yes' and when to say 'no'.

Some examples:
- I never lend money, not even to my best friends.
- I take half an hour for myself every day.
- I check my emails only four times each day.
- I never make appointments on a Thursday evening, because that is my tennis evening.
- Sunday is family day, when I enjoy my partner and the kids.
- I make an appointment at the hairdressers' once every five weeks, because I want to take care of myself and my appearance.

» I always turn my phone off during meals. I want to enjoy my food and the nourishment it gives my body.

SAYING NO IS IMPORTANT FOR YOUR SUCCESS

Freddy is self-employed. He has been running a successful shoe shop for years. In recent times, his business has grown fast, so that he has now decided to follow coaching 'to get some order back in my mind', as he puts it rather nicely. During one of our coaching sessions, he enters all flustered and immediately starts his story.
'There's mountains of paperwork and the wages need to be paid, but I keep getting disturbed all the time.'
'So what can you do to stop being disturbed?' I ask.
'That's just not possible. My staff are standing at my desk every five minutes.'
'And what if you don't allow it? What if you just say "no" for once?'
'That's not possible, either. They need me for everything.'
'Really? Are you sure?'
Freddy keeps on finding excuses but I won't let go. I keep on asking him how he can do things differently. Suddenly, I see Freddy's face light up. He has found a simple solution. 'I'm going to shut my office door for two hours each day, so that I can work in peace. And I'm going to inform my people that I don't want to be disturbed when my door is closed.'

Why is saying 'no' so difficult?

This has a lot to do with our upbringing. As a child, you quickly learned that saying 'no' was not done. If you said 'no', if you refused to do something, it would have been possible to get punished. If you said 'yes', if you agreed to do something, the face of the person making the request lit up with pleasure. It was even possible that you got rewarded. In other words, we are taught at an early age not to say 'no'. Which means that it is not surprising that we still

The 'no' you say to someone else is often a 'yes' to yourself.

find it difficult to say 'no', even when we are grown up. But the 'no' you say to someone else is often a 'yes' to yourself. If, by the end of the week, you have been able to do everything you wanted to do because you regularly said 'no', you can justifiably reward yourself. You earned it.

Just imagine the objectives you could reach if you regularly say 'no'. When you build 'me' moments into your daily routine, there is a good chance that you will be more productive at other moments of the day. You will feel more satisfied, will give your body and mind the rest they sometimes need, and, as a result, will be more in balance.

Businessmen like Freddy learn from hard experience how important it is to say 'no'. And there is nothing wrong with that, if you do it in a responsible way.

You can learn how to say 'no'. After all, you can't meet three deadlines all at the same time, can you? You can't do your work and the work of your colleagues as well. You can't answer all your emails instantly. Just look at your agenda. But imagine if the hours you have wasted today on time-consuming and non-productive matters could be transformed into productive hours. What might you achieve?

Saying 'no' is an important step on the road to success!

FIND YOUR PERSONAL 'NO'

There are different ways to say 'no'. Try to find the way that suits you best. Perhaps this is it: 'Thank you for your kind invitation, but I just made another engagement'. Or maybe: 'No, I'm afraid I can't make it tonight. I promised myself that I would only cancel my tennis evening in a real emergency. Can we meet tomorrow or some other time?' You don't always even need to give a reason. Your appointment with yourself is just as important – perhaps more important – than the appointment you are turning down. Does your friend keep on sending you silly jokes by sms, which take hours to read each day? Tell him you appreciate him

Saying 'no' is a form of self-preservation. Often, we don't want to hurt the other person's feelings, but what good does that do us?

thinking of you in this way, but could he perhaps cut down their number to something more reasonable?

Saying 'no' is a form of self-preservation. Often, we don't want to hurt the other person's feelings, but what good does that do us? What's more, it is often easier for others if you say 'no' straight away, rather than saying 'yes' and then changing your mind or not being able to do what you promised.

'MUST' MAKES YOU TIRED

We can take things a step further. We often have the feeling that we 'must' do certain things, so that we feel it is not right to say 'no'. But is that always true? We could say that we might, can or will do these things. Or we can choose to do them or not do them: in other words, consciously say either 'yes' or 'no' with 100% conviction. The word 'must' can weigh heavily on our unconscious mind. If, however, you are aware that you always have a choice, you will be able to pass through life more easily.

Bruce, the manager of a company we have been working with for years, stuck to his guns.
'Surely we must work, mustn't we?'
I had my answer ready. 'It's not a question of "must". It's a question of wanting to, because you like the money work brings in. If you don't want to work, you would have to face the financial consequences.'
'Okay', he concedes. One-nil for you. He tries again. 'But we must eat?'
'No, it's the same thing. You don't have to eat, you want to eat. Your body needs food; otherwise you would have to face the consequences of starvation.'
Two-nil.
'But surely you agree that I must take care of my staff at work?' says Bruce triumphantly. This time, he thinks he's got me.
'You really think so?' I ask doubtfully. 'Or is that not just another example of something you want to do rather than must do? What would happen if you didn't take

care of them? What would be the consequences: for the company, for yourself...?'

Bruce looks at me and nods. Game, set and match.

'Shall we start the training again?' I ask him.

'I suppose so... if we must,' he replies with a smile.

How often do you use the word 'must'? Now that you have learned that this little word undermines the working of your unconscious brain, we would advise you to avoid it wherever possible. Just give it a try. You can easily replace 'must' with words like 'going to', 'will', 'want to', 'would like to', etc.

We frequently hear people say things like: 'We have worked hard this week, so we really must organize a party to celebrate!'

Hello? You are talking about a party: having fun, laughing, meeting friends, dancing... If this is something you 'must' do, then it is no longer a party; it is an obligation, which means it will also drain you of energy. This is a subject we like to discuss during our trainings. The reactions we get are many and varied, such as: 'We can't let our friends down'; 'They expect us to come'; or 'If you're invited, you must go...'

Why 'must' you? In our opinion, there is no 'must' about it. If you go to a party, it's because you want to. You are responsible for your own life and you shouldn't let others lead it for you. If you turn the invitation down – in other words, if you say 'no' – think about the possible consequences. Will your friends be angry with you? Will they feel insulted? Will they never want to see you again? In most cases, none of these things are likely to happen. If you explain clearly why you can't come on this occasion, they will usually understand. In matters of this kind, it is always better to be honest than to give a false excuse.

'YOU MUST...' SAYS WHO?

Mia is going through a difficult patch in her life. She has the feeling that the whole world is on her shoulders. Too much work at the office, a husband who is often away from home, the children who need driving everywhere during her 'free' time... It's all getting a bit too much for her – something she already mentioned once or twice in previous sessions.

She no longer feels in control, but nobody seems able to notice it. If she talks about it to friends, they don't really take her seriously. Surely she has nothing to complain about: good job, nice husband, great kids...? Mia feels trapped in a vicious circle. In the past, she used to enjoy a good night out with the girls, but arranging a babysitter has become such a hassle that she now thinks 'Why bother?' and prefers to stay at home.

And things are going from bad to worse. She is becoming irritable, thinks she is letting people down at work, no longer feels as though she is a good wife and mother...

She tells me how her husband came home one evening and announced enthusiastically that their friends had organized a surprise party, to which they were invited. He was really looking forward to going.

Mia looks at me.

'I didn't know what to say. I had hoped we could just have a quite weekend, but now it seemed as though our social life had also become an obligation. I summoned up all my courage and told him what I felt; that I was exhausted; that life was getting me down, at least for the moment. The tears began to roll down my cheeks and he put a comforting arm around my shoulder. This one kind gesture made it possible for me to pour out everything that had been on my mind for months. I just couldn't stop talking...

We frequently make life more difficult for ourselves than is necessary. By talking about the things we need to talk about, by making clear agreements with others and by refusing to always be told that we 'must', we can put much less stress on our system, which in the long term can only make us feel better. What's more, you can use this technique in all areas of your life. Once again, body and mind are part of the same story. Even a fun activity can become an obligation if we feel tired. At that moment, your body will let you know that it has had enough. Unfortunately, we often fail to listen to the body when we are dealing with matters of 'must'. As a result, the body gets even more tired and the mind gets more and more signals that this or that 'must' be done, rather than wanting to do them. It is only by breaking this vicious circle that you will be able to give your body the rest it needs and release the pressure on your thoughts. Only then will the tension slowly fade away.

> *Even a fun activity can become an obligation if we are feeling tired.*

YES, I WANT TO...!

'I just want to take a quick breath of fresh air during my lunch break.'
'I want to help Bert with moving house.'
'I am going to make something nice to eat this evening.'
'I'll call in at the rest home on my way back; that'll be nice for my mother.'
'I am leaving for work.'
'I would like to help the children with their homework.'

You could use the word 'must' in all these sentences. Just give it a try. You will notice how much 'heavier' the sentences become. You can practice this alternative use of words in the sentences you use every day, at home and at work. Just ask yourself how you can word your 'must' sentences differently.

First check whether the subject of the sentence is really something that you 'must' do. If it is, ask who says so. You will frequently find that you are the only person who thinks that it 'must'. In other words, you are doing all this to yourself. Are you sure you are right when you say that it must? How about being a little kinder to yourself and not committing yourself to so much obligations? There are lots of things you can 'want' to do, and that creates a more relaxed and easy living, even though you end up doing exactly the same things.

Words like 'no', 'must' and 'yes, I want to' can make a world of difference.

Coach yourself!

Do you take enough time for yourself? How exactly, in concrete terms?

Do you have a list of things that are important for you and your wellbeing? How does this list help you to say 'no'?

What ways of saying 'no' have you already tried?

How often do you use the word 'must'? Who says that you must? And why?

How does it feel for you if you replace 'must' with a friendlier verb?

Write down the insights to take with you for your director's diploma.

....

....

....

....

....

....

....

....

....

GET YOUR FRAMES STRAIGHT
Learn to set boundaries

Note to the director
In the previous chapter, we learned how to make clear what we want and, above all, what we don't want. In this chapter, we will discover how to create a framework that makes this clear to others and indicates where your boundaries lie. This will make your life a whole lot easier, especially if you are a leader.

Are you a business leader, working with a team? If so, you will probably recognize the following story. It shows that it is not easy to keep your team motivated, whilst at the same time setting your own boundaries.

We are sitting in the coaching practice with Anna, a young entrepreneur who recently set up a new company in the heart of New York. In other words, she is a woman with guts. Even so, during one of our coaching sessions she made a surprising confession.

Anna: 'To be honest, I don't find it easy to play the "boss".'
She makes quotation marks in the air with her hands when she says the word 'boss'.
'I've noticed that my team doesn't always do what I want, but I find it so difficult to point this out to them. We're all about the same age and I don't want to put myself above them. But this means they sometimes feel free to do their own thing. Don't misunderstand me; in general, they do a great job. It's the little things: lunch breaks, messy desks,…'

Anna's situation is by no means unique. On the contrary: lots of leaders, especially younger ones, struggle with this problem. Nowadays 'freedom' and 'enjoy yourself' are the new buzzwords. 'Rules' are a thing of the past, we don't have to follow them. If everyone takes his responsibility seriously, things will turn out alright in the end.

This all sounds fine, but if everyone just does whatever they want, does things the way he/she believes they should be done, this can only lead to confusion and, in a worst-case scenario, to chaos. You might think it is important to tidy up the office at the end of the day, while I see disorder as a sign of creativity. You might scrupulously put your dirty cups in the dishwasher, whereas I might regard this as a waste of my valuable time, which I should use on more productive tasks.

> *If everyone just does whatever they want, does things the way he/she believes they should be done, this can only lead to confusion or, in a worst-case scenario, to chaos.*

This can lead to tensions of all kinds, great and small.

It is important as a leader that you are clear about certain rules; that you are consistent in their application; and that you make no exceptions. It is what it is: for everyone. This asks plenty of discipline from the leader, but it is well worth it in the long run. Your team will soon get used to your rules, so that they eventually become second nature. To begin with, you may need to check quite regularly that the rules are being respected, but once the system is up and running you will soon notice that there is more time in the office for the things that really count. And you will also see that in most cases rules actually lead to more freedom, not less.

All too often, we assume that other people will react the way we want them to react. That they will see things the way we see them, will behave the way we would behave, will follow the rules that we would find reasonable to follow. Nothing could be further from the truth.

Never base your actions on assumptions. If you do, you are likely to end up disappointed. So how can you avoid misunderstandings? By making crystal clear exactly what you want.

 A few months ago, I was phoned by Tom, the owner of a clothes shop. He asked me to coach him through a trajectory that would help him to get better results from his staff. He had no doubts about the scale of the task. 'Believe me, there's a hell of a lot of work that needs to be done. I've got this new girl, Marie, but she can't even make the coffee right.'

A few weeks later, as promised, I pay a visit to his shop. While I am waiting for Tom, a young woman approaches me and asks if I would like something to drink. I instantly know that this is the new girl Marie, about whom Tom had been talking. I ask for a coffee and a few minutes later she returns with a steaming cup, which she hands over with a friendly smile. I take a sip and can't understand what Tom meant with his remarks: it is delicious!

When Tom arrives, we go and sit in his office. He also asks me if I would like a drink and I again ask for coffee. When he places this new cup in front of me, I can immediately understand what he meant about Marie. Tom's cup is served on a small tray, with the spoon, sugar, milk and biscuit all neatly lined up alongside each other. There is even a little bowl with a chocolate in it. With Marie, there was no tray, no biscuit and no chocolate, and the milk and sugar were just propped on the edge of the saucer.

So there is clearly a difference, but this leads to an interesting question: where does the problem lie – with Tom or with Marie?

If you want everything to run like clockwork in your company, the main responsibility for making this happen rests with you, the leader. The way you train your people will ultimately determine just how successful you are.

 If you want to teach others new things, there are four stages you will need to go through. Test it for yourself; you will soon notice that it works.

If you want everything to run like clockwork in your company, the main responsibility for making this happen rests with you, the leader.

Step 1: Demonstrate

Show people what you want them to learn. Your staff first need to see exactly what you mean before they can understand it. Ask them if everything is clear; if not, start again.

If Tom had given Marie a demonstration of how he wants coffee to be served in his shop, she would have been better aware of what he expects from her.

By now, you might be thinking: 'Do I really need to do that for everything in my company?' The answer is 'yes', if it is necessary.

Step 2: Repeat

Let your staff perform the same task, so they can show you they understood. Be honest with them about the result. If you are not satisfied, say so.

Step 3: Practice

Practice is often necessary. Give the staff time to improve their skills. Remember that they will probably still make mistakes in this early phase. Remember also that when there is not enough practice things can seriously go wrong. You can't be a real expert until you have done the same things thousands of times. Just ask any top sportsman or -woman.

Step 4: Again

If things are still not going the way you want during the practice phase, it is best to start all over again.

Demonstrate–repeat–practice–again. Compare it with a game. You might have played a game for years, but you still keep making mistakes. It is only by constant practice and playing that you will eventually make it to the next level. And it's not different in real life...

KNOW YOUR FRAMES

Getting your frames – your frames of reference – straight can help your team to work in a more streamlined manner, allowing them to focus on the things that are most important for you and the company. Of course, it is vital to know precisely what your own frames of reference are. What is okay and what is not okay? Where is the boundary of what is acceptable? Once you are clear in your own mind about these things, it is crucial to notify them clearly to your team and to initiate the four-step process outlined above. This requires discipline and perseverance from everyone, including you, the leader. Because if you don't stick to the rules, why should anyone else? Far too often we see problems arise because of the inconsistency and backsliding of the people at the top. And that's a real shame...

 Coach yourself!

When you think about your work, which uncertainties and ambiguities confuse you?
How do you teach things to others?
Do you know your own frames of reference?
How are they linked to your drivers?
What can you do to get your frames straight?
How do you like to receive instructions?
Learn from this when you are giving instructions to others.
Practice the four-step method of learning. What do you think of this method?
Write down the insights to take with you for your director's diploma.

....

....

....

....

....

4. TOGETHER WE ARE STRONG

In the previous chapters, we have learned how to keep control over our own life. In part, we do this by communicating with others in the right manner, from the very depths of our being.

We have now reached the point where we have achieved balance in our life. We are confident that we will be able to reach our final objectives. We know that we can be happy and successful, if not yet then at least in the future.

But people are never happy and successful in isolation. It is only by sharing with others that we can continue to learn and grow. It is input from others that will make your drivers and objectives increasingly clear.

LOOK AT WHAT OTHERS CAN GIVE YOU
Life is about giving and receiving. So make sure you receive!

Note to the director
Never stand still in life, because the world keeps on turning. Continue to learn, your whole life long, and enrich yourself with new experiences. And you don't need to look too far, because the people around you have a lot to offer. All you need is the openness and the willingness to accept it.

Imagine you are going on holiday. Surely it is the most normal thing in the world to ask your neighbour to water your plants and feed the cat while you are away? Or are you one of those people who think that it is 'not done' to ask for others for help?

Louise is sitting in front of me, her leg resting on a stool after a serious operation on her foot. I ask her what she wants to talk about today.

'Perhaps where I can get a new foot,' she jokes. 'To be honest, the pain in my foot is not too bad. I can deal with that. But organizing things at home: that's another matter.'

I know Louise as a real career woman: fast, efficient and result-oriented. I suppose it's only to be expected that being forced to sit at home for a couple of weeks is getting to her. 'You know, I'm always ready to help anyone, but now that it's my turn to need a bit of help…' Her voice chokes with a sob.

'So what happens then?' I ask her, full of curiosity.

'Nothing, that's what happens. I'm just left to get on with things by myself.'

'Nobody? Completely left on your own?' I repeat.

'Yes. I suppose I shouldn't expect that someone will do something for me. Or my kids.' Louise is clearly very angry.

'And have you asked anyone?'

'No, of course not. You can't ask things like that!'

'Really,' I say amazed. 'That's news to me. Why can't you ask?'

'Because I assume that anyone who is my friend will do it automatically.'

Louise's reasoning is totally wrong. So be on your guard against it. Don't assume that others will know when they can help you. You have to ask them. They don't have a crystal ball and they can't read your mind. So let them know.

People like to help each other. That's the way it's always been and that's the way it will stay. By nature, we human beings are social creatures, who function best in a group. Helping each other is part of who we are. But we have all kinds of

If you understand that life is a matter of both giving and receiving, accept the fact that from time to time it's going to be your turn to receive.

prejudices when it comes to asking for the help we need. We think that people will judge or that we should really be able to manage by ourselves. We doubt and hesitate, before finally deciding that there must be some other way around the problem.

But if you understand that life is a matter of both giving and receiving, accept the fact that from time to time it's going to be your turn to receive.

LEARNING FROM OTHERS

Allowing ourselves to be helped is one thing, but do you also realize how much you can learn from other people? It is becoming increasingly important to know that you can do this at all times, in all places and at all ages. The world is changing rapidly and information is getting ever more complex. The things we learned at school are becoming less and less relevant. If we want to keep up, we need to keep on learning new things all the time.

Allowing ourselves to be helped is one thing, but do you also realize how much you can learn from other people?

Companies are applying this principle with ever greater frequency, with the younger generation now being systematically used to re-educate their 'elders'. It's known as 'reverse coaching'. For example, a young twenty-something might teach an older co-worker about some extra tricks in social media.

If you want to learn from others, you need to open yourself up completely to their help. This means taking every opportunity, whenever it arises, without judgement. Never refuse.

If you open up this way, you will be amazed at what you can still learn from 'the school of life'.

 Patrick rings the bell. I open the door with pleasure. A powerful man stands before me. 57 years old, intelligent, business-like, well spoken: that's Patrick. He has been running his own successful company for decades.

A few sessions ago, he let it slip that he felt he knew fewer and fewer answers than in the past. As a result, he started to doubt his own leadership qualities. He put it down to getting older. In particular, he blamed himself for one or two poor recent decisions (which, nota bene, he had not actually made himself). He started to question himself.

Today, three sessions later, I can immediately feel that he is full of new energy as he walks into my office.

'I've done it. I've found the solution.' He almost gives himself a congratulatory pat on the back.

'That sounds great!' I say encouragingly.

'Last time, you were very clear and I understood your message. So the next day I made the click. I've had enough of wallowing in self-pity. I called together my managers and asked them to tell me the biggest problems they face. At first, they were surprised, but soon enough a few of them were very open and honest, which I appreciated. After that, we brainstormed about the best possible solutions. It soon became clear that in every department we have someone – usually one of the younger employees – with the crucial knowledge we are currently lacking. But we are just not using them properly. So we agreed to make the necessary organizational changes, and do you know what?' He pauses for dramatic effect, with a broad grin on his face. 'I never knew I had such talent in the company! The younger generation has suddenly stepped up to the plate and they have a very different kind of knowledge from me and my managers. So now everyone is happy, and we'll soon see it in the balance sheet as well!'

Search for the talents in other people. If you think that someone talks well, listen to them as often as you can. If you know someone who can look at things more rationally than you do, ask her how she does it. There are opportunities to learn every day – so don't miss your chance!

THE ETERNAL STUDENT

Learning from others has become a constant. Ask yourself as well what you might be able to teach to someone else. We sometimes forget what we have learned or are able to do. In coaching terminology this is known as 'unconscious competence'. You have done certain things for years, more or less on automatic pilot, but you have forgotten how you ever learned it. Consider, for example, brushing your teeth. This is something that you do every day, almost without thinking, but you have no idea how you first came to learn it.

The learning process works in both directions. So what can you do that others cannot (yet) do? Sometimes, it can be very simple things. Here are some examples:

» Thanks to your wide ranging travel experience, you know how to get through the security control at airports quickly and efficiently. For example, you never wear a belt if you are travelling abroad by plane.
» Thanks to the internship you once did in a clothes store, you know how to fold a shirt perfectly.
» You know which shortcut keys to use, so that you can write a memo twice as fast.
» As a result of your years of yoga lessons, you know different breathing techniques that can calm you down and bring you peace.
» You know that it is better not to use a red or green pen when writing on a flip chart, because some people are colour-blind for those colours.
» After working all your life in R&D, you know which materials best retain heat. As a result you bought a cup in a material that will keep your coffee warm during your long car rides to the office.
» You know the best way to peel an onion without cutting your fingers.
» ...

Carry on learning from others, and be aware of what you might be able to teach them.

Coach yourself!

How do you allow yourself to be helped by others?
How do you make clear to others what you really need from them?
How do you ensure that you learn from every moment of every day?
What do you want to learn from people who are younger than you?
Can you describe two or three things that you could learn from people in your immediate surroundings?
Can you describe two or three things that you could teach to others?
Write down the insights to take with you for your director's diploma.

(NET)WORKING TOGETHER
Together, we can go to the next level

 Note to the director

In this chapter, we will look more closely at networking and working together with others. But because we don't want to talk about networking in the narrow sense of the word, we will use the term 'networking together'. Or how you can discover that one and one makes three, or in time even three thousand. In the following pages, you will need to use all the skills and techniques you have learned in this book so far. But if you succeed, you will be ready to take the leading role – the director's role – in your life. And this is something you will do together with others – because (let's admit it) that is much more fascinating than doing it alone. But at all times you remain firmly seated in the director's chair. And you will be amazed by what you can now achieve!

In our final visit to the coaching practice, we meet Boris, the owner of a large building company. He leads a busy life, constantly rushing from one place to another to make sure that everything is going according to plan on site, as well as keeping in close contact with his customers and suppliers. For Boris, networking events in the evening are something of a necessary evil. They are not really his cup of tea at all…

 'I hate having to go to all those networking events, but for me that's the only way to meet a lot of new potential customers in a short time. But I really dislike doing it and I never quite know how to behave. So I just stand there, leaning on one of those high tables, ready to give my sales pitch whenever anyone asks me. But I always feel very uncomfortable and can hardly wait to get out of the place. How come some people find it so easy and I find it so hard?'

What Boris is experiencing is not abnormal. Many people have the same feeling when they attend an open networking event. They are seized by panic, because they feel that they 'must' speak to other people. But this is looking at networking in the very narrow sense of the word: literally, a kind of rigged game with unwritten rules of behaviour, where people pay to get the chance to talk to other people.

When this happens, networking becomes an objective in its own right, part of the job... This leads to unnatural conversations and unnatural reactions, from which concrete results (an appointment for a further meeting, a deal, etc.) sometimes arise and sometimes don't.

Thousands of books have already been written about the do's and don'ts of this kind of networking. But we want to talk about a different kind of networking, a networking that doesn't take what you do as its starting point, but focuses instead on who you are.

> Boris is still looking puzzled, so I ask him: 'Are there also moments when you do find it easy to make spontaneous contact with other people?'
> 'Of course,' he answers, 'but that's usually in my private life. For example, when I go to a concert with my wife. Then I feel really at ease and it often happens that I start chatting to people during the interval. I think I also enjoy it more because it's something I'm able to share with my wife. At a proper networking event, I usually feel guilty, because I'm spending yet another night away from home.'

Boris experiences a huge difference between 'networking' for his professional activities and 'networking' at a concert. This is because music is one of his passions; it gives him energy, which he spontaneously wishes to share with others. He also feels more comfortable because he has someone at his side whom he trusts and loves. What Boris needs to see is that there should be no difference between the two different forms of networking. If you don't look at networking as 'work', but see it instead as a habit that you build into your daily life, networking then becomes networking together. Or at least it will, on condition that in your daily life you can occupy yourself with things that also fill you with passion and energy. Sounds complex? Here are a few words of explanation.

YOU NEED TO NETWORK FROM THE DEPTH OF YOUR BEING

Let's begin at the beginning: how can we define networking in the broad sense of the word? You could describe it as 'having around you at every moment of your life people who can support you and whom you can support'. And to make things perfectly clear, this is not limited to the professional environment. It applies equally, for example, to another mother you can call to pick up your kids from school, if you are held up at work. Or a neighbour you can ask if he knows a good bricklayer, because you want to build a new wall in your back garden.

To build up such a network around you, it is important that you are able to 'connect' with others. You need to let them know that you can mean something for them, so that they will be ready to gladly do something for you, if you ask. But you can only create this kind of confidence and trust if you approach others on the basis of who you are, not what you do.

This is one of the most common mistakes made at professional networking events. People approach each other first and foremost because of what they do. This is easy, because on the badge you get when you enter, the name of your company and your function are often printed in larger letters than your own name. This points people in a particular direction. Once the first introductions have been made, the next logical questions are: 'Who do you work for?', 'What do you do?', 'How long?', 'What do you need?', etc. In return, you get answers like 'I work there', 'I sell that', etc.

When there is no immediate match of interests, the conversation quickly starts to peter out; eyes look away, listening becomes perfunctory, bodies are turned to get a better view of the room and other perspective 'targets'. Using standard polite excuses like 'I think I'll just get another drink' or 'I think I can see an old colleague over there', the conversation comes to an end and the group breaks up. Everyone knows that these excuses are not genuine, but nobody seems to mind. It's all just part of the networking game.

Let's be clear on this point: there is absolutely nothing wrong with professional networking events. But if you attend one, make sure you approach it the right way – otherwise it will be a complete waste of your valuable time. Remember our friend Boris, who felt guilty about exchanging quality time with his wife for an evening of swapping business cards with people he didn't know. Our advice to Boris was this: 'If collecting business cards is all you get out of your networking evening, you would do better just to stay at home and curl up on the couch with your wife and a good bottle of wine. From a business perspective, you can spend your time more usefully accessing database lists of potential customers with a specific interest in your product.'

So how do you do that, connecting with others from the depth of your being? And why is it so different? You will experience the difference yourself when you consciously give it a try. Imagine that you run a company selling gift items. You are at a trade fair and you get into conversation with someone you don't know. You could talk about how long you have had the business, what type of gifts you sell, where the company is based, etc. Alternatively, you could take 'why' as your starting point: you can tell your visitor why you do what you do. This immediately launches you into a very different story. Your answer to the question 'What do you do?' might now be: 'I make people happy'. With an answer like this, the conversation can quickly move in unexpected directions. 'Oh yes, and how do you make them happy? I also want to be happy, so tell me.' You see? From here, your conversation might lead anywhere.

Now imagine that you are a health coach and someone asks you: 'What do you do?' A logical answer might be: 'I am a health coach'. Informative? Not very. So why not try something like: 'I live healthily, I like laughing and sometimes I colour outside the lines'. In this way, you illustrate what you do in relation to your inner being, to who you really are. This is more likely to engage the curiosity of your listener, so that he will be even more interested when he learns later on in the conversation that you are a health coach, because he has already had a first-hand example of how you approach your professional activities.

Give it a try.

NETWORKING IS GIVING AND RECEIVING

There is another popular misconception about 'networking': namely, that it is about giving and receiving, but with receiving rather than giving being the main objective. We are here to tell you that this doesn't work. It will only work if the giving and the receiving are equally important. At classic networking events, you can sometimes be left with the feeling that you have listened to ten different stories, but that nobody has listened to yours. Whereas we know that this is what people really want: to be listened to. So if you want to connect with people, the secret is simple: just listen.

If you want to connect with people, the secret is simple: just listen.

We have already discussed how you should do this in 'Doing for dummies'. Make sure you use the technique whenever you network.

Engage yourself fully in the conversation. Ask 'interesting' questions. Try to get your conversation partner to open up: 'What brings you here?', 'What makes you unique?', 'What is the most interesting thing you have heard here so far tonight?', 'What is the most important thing that I need to know about you?' These are not standard questions, so the chance that you will get a standard answer is pretty small.

In other words, it's all about the attitude with which you approach the conversation. Try and explore the interesting side of your conversation partner. Find ways to discover how you might be able to help him. Find ways to discover how he might be able to help you. Giving and receiving. The rest will automatically follow.

NETWORKING: ALWAYS AND EVERYWHERE

We have already encouraged you not to confine your networking to classic networking events. Networking is something you should make a habit of in your everyday life, something you do always and everywhere. Search constantly for opportunities to receive things: at the baker's, on the train, from your colleagues. And don't forget the possibilities for online networking that exist today: social media, communities on specific themes, etc.

You can also consciously create 'out of the box' networking opportunities. For example, you can go to a book presentation on a subject that interests you, but has nothing to do with your professional activities. Who knows who you will meet or what you will discover. Or you could invite people who you find interesting for a roundtable discussion on a particular theme. Or make your showroom available to young people with talent, as a place where they can display their work. You will be amazed how often new opportunities arise from totally unexpected quarters. You will also see that the more passionately you are engaged with the things you do, the easier it becomes to network spontaneously.

This is also logical. If you are passionate about your work, it will not easily let you go. Not even when you are on holiday. If you are a fashion designer on vacation in Italy, you will almost certainly take note of the way the Italians dress. You will want to visit more clothes shops than the average tourist. You might even ask a passing local if the beautiful scarf she is wearing is of Italian design. If you are really lucky, perhaps she is just as passionate about fashion as you are. And then you are off and running. Who knows where such a conversation might lead to?

The more passionately you are engaged with the things you do, the easier it becomes to network spontaneously.

YOUR ELEVATOR PITCH

Once you know that networking is something you can do always and everywhere, you need to be prepared to seize the opportunities when they arise. That's why it's a good idea to regularly have another look at your identity card, so you can identify the elements you want to share with others.

You can turn these elements into a kind of introductory speech, sometimes known as an elevator pitch, with a short version and a long version. What do you want people to know about you? We have already looked at the example of 'I make people happy'. You could extend that with something like: 'Nowadays, people seldom stop to think what it means to give something to someone else'. And then: 'With my gift articles, I give people the chance to show their gratitude to others'.

FROM NETWORKING TO NETWORKING TOGETHER

There is a superlative form of networking: networking together. You won't find this phrase anywhere in a dictionary, because it goes beyond simple rationality. Networking together goes much further than the standard idea of interaction or collaboration: it is about trust, about values, about intuition, about giving yourself, and about getting so much in return.

When you network with someone, it is possible that your values are wholly incompatible. If you then decide to collaborate, your partnership is unlikely to last for very long, because your values are so different. When you network together with someone, this will be much more difficult if the values, convictions and world view of the other person are not the same as your own. Why? Because in networking together we need to be able to trust the other person completely, and this is impossible if he or she has a totally different view of life. Your intention is to work together for a common objective. This means that you are going to share many different things, often without getting much in return, but knowing that the end result will still be better. But how will this work if you don't even share the same basic values?

If we say that your values need to be wholly compatible with your networking together partner, this does not mean that the two of you cannot be different.

If we say that your values need to be wholly compatible with your networking together partner, this does not mean that the two of you cannot be different. It is perfectly possible that the other person is in a different field of business to yours and that your characters are also different. When we talk about compatability, we are talking about your deeper being, about the core that remains once all the outer layers have been stripped away. This is where you need to find your points of common ground.

WHY WE FIND NETWORKING TOGETHER SO DIFFICULT

A lot of people find it difficult to network together. In part, this is connected with cultural background. Because networking together is essentially about sharing, and this is something we were never taught at school. Nor is it an important part of the culture in the business world.

Our current society is still much too firmly focused on 'rational knowledge'. At school, we are evaluated for what we know. At work, we are similarly valued for our knowledge. If I know something that you don't know, you need me and will value me (or rather, my knowledge). According to this reasoning, I am unlikely to easily share that knowledge, because this would diminish my own worth and privileged status.

Networking together takes a completely different starting point. You are willing to share ideas with the other person, because you know you can learn from the other person how to make those ideas better for everyone, perhaps because his strengths are different from your strengths. You trust that the other person will do everything together with you to achieve a better end result, without him running away with your idea.

At the same time, you will also do everything in your power to help the other person to achieve better results. This does not necessarily mean that you will immediately receive something similar or equivalent in return. But you are prepared to apply the 'pay-it-forward' principle. You trust that everything you give, and the manner in which you give it, will sooner or later, in one way or another, be given back to you in a form that is at least equally fine.

FROM ME TO WE

We began this chapter by saying that the best thing you can do is to develop the habit of networking together, always and everywhere. This goes far beyond simple 'networking' as it is usually understood in professional circles.

If everyone would be open enough to share their strengths with others and to trust in the strengths of others when they are clearly better, the result would be much more creative companies and many more people with smiling faces than there are now. In this way, personal leadership can lead to collective leadership.

Today, we still live far too much in a 'me'-focused culture, where top qualifications, a top job and finding your own way to the top are still the highest good. It is every man for himself. But the world has become too complex to carry on this way. The simple linear solutions of the past are no longer able to answer the complicated problems of the present and the future. We need each other and each other's knowledge if we want to survive. We must evolve from a 'me'-culture to a 'we'-culture. By combining our strengths, we can arrive at the creative solutions the world so desperately needs. If everyone goes in search of the unique contribution that he or she can make to this process, a new form of collective leadership can be developed. Everyone will play their own authentic role in the great project in which we are all involved: to make the world a better place. This is what we believe: if we want to make progress, we must make a commitment to reinvent ourselves in the light of the networking together ideal.

> **Coach yourself!**
>
> How do you network on the basis of who you are?
> What is your introductory 'elevator pitch'?
> What do you need before you can give with trust?
> How can you evolve from networking to networking together?
> How can you make your unique contribution towards 'real' networking together with others?

DIRECTOR'S EXAM*

In 'I do' you learned about the skills that are necessary if you want to live your life in keeping with who you really are. You can also see it as the range of skills you need to get your director's diploma.

Give yourself a score for the questions on the following pages and try to think how you might improve these scores in the future. But remember: your final score in this exam is not important. What is important is your improvement plan.

1. How much of who I really am do I currently show at work?
Score: 1   2   3   4   5   6   7   8   9   10

How can I show more of my true self to others at work?

....

....

....

....

....

* For an electronic version, mail us at info@qlick.today

2. How well do I look after my body?

Score: 1 2 3 4 5 6 7 8 9 10

What more can I do to look after my body?

....

....

....

....

3. How pure are my thoughts on an average working day?

Score: 1 2 3 4 5 6 7 8 9 10

What can I do to make these thoughts even purer?

....

....

....

....

4. How effective is my communication with others?

Score: 1 2 3 4 5 6 7 8 9 10

What can I do to make my communication even more effective?

....

....

....

....

5. How well do I listen?
Score: 1 2 3 4 5 6 7 8 9 10

What can I do to listen – really listen – more closely to others?

....

....

....

....

6. How often do I give feedback to nourish others?
Score: 1 2 3 4 5 6 7 8 9 10

Where and when can I give more feedback?

....

....

....

....

7. How do I react to the feedback I get from others?
Score: 1 2 3 4 5 6 7 8 9 10

What can I do to receive this feedback with greater openness?

....

....

....

....

8. How great is my impact on my surroundings?
Score: 1 2 3 4 5 6 7 8 9 10

What can I do to increase my impact on the people and things around me?

....

....

....

9. How efficient am I currently in (net)working together with others?
Score: 1 2 3 4 5 6 7 8 9 10

What can I do to improve my (net)working together in the future?

....

....

....

10. How much have I learned from this book?
Score: 1 2 3 4 5 6 7 8 9 10

What can I do and where can I find information to learn more?

....

....

....

To get your diploma, mail your answers to us at info@qlick.today

FINALLY: GOOD LUCK WITH YOUR PREMIERE!

You have now followed the complete coaching trajectory in this book. You should now have all the tools you need to continue your journey happily and with confidence. But we don't want to let you go without a last few pieces of good advice. Because it doesn't stop here. Personal leadership means that you need to keep on coaching yourself continually. So imprint the following tips firmly on your mind. Cut them out. Hang them on a board over your bed. It doesn't matter what you do, as long as you look at them regularly. Even better, plan it in your agenda, because it is one of your most important tasks for the rest of your life.

1. Give yourself a regular upgrade
The world is changing rapidly, so make sure that you don't stand still. Follow professional (re-)training as often as you can, but also be open to learn from others every single day. Try to look at the world with an open mind, with the wonderment of a child, and without prejudices or preconceptions. Dare to ask questions: it is the easiest way to learn.

2. Download the new version of yourself in good time
Don't hang on to the same old thoughts. Dust them down or change them regularly. Perhaps what you thought three years ago is no longer relevant. Be aware that you are constantly evolving, as a result of your daily experiences and meetings with others. Make sure that what you do continues to be in line with who you are. Make equally sure that the same is true in your relations with others, your work, your hobbies. If you notice that something somewhere is not quite right, download a new version of yourself.

3. Dare to jump in time

Dare to take action promptly. Dreaming is fine, but if all you do is dream nothing is ever going to happen. So make sure you press the play button in time. It will sometimes be necessary to take difficult decisions, sometimes with serious consequences. Trust your gut feeling. Don't be too impulsive, but also remember that taking no decision is often worse than taking a bad decision. You can at least learn from a bad decision and try again.

4. Pause to enjoy your successes

There is nothing wrong with always wanting to do better. There is nothing wrong with failure either, as long as you learn from it. Above all, don't forget to stop and enjoy your successes when they come along. Give yourself a well-deserved pat on the back. When you have achieved something, take a breather, recharge your batteries and drink a glass of champagne. You will then be ready to start again, with the bar set even higher. This not only programmes your brain in a positive manner, but will also increase the recognition of others for what you do.

5. Keep on valuing yourself

Remember to value yourself sufficiently highly: you are the only one who really can. Never devalue your own worth and don't persist in comparing yourself to others. Your main concern, both inside and outside, is: 'Where is my core and how can I use it to make the world a better place?'

Trust in who you are, because you are your greatest contribution to the world!

THANK YOU

Thank you for having the courage and taking the time to read this book.

Thank you to all our coachees and trainees for their confidence in us and in Qlick.

Thank you to our colleagues for their inspiration.

Thank you to everyone we have met along our path, who allowed us to both give and receive.

Thank you to our families and friends for always being there for us.

Would you like to know more about the authors?
Take a look at www.qlick.today.